THE YEAR YO
WERE BORN
1952

A fascinating book about the year 1952 with information on:
Events of the year UK, Adverts of 1952, Cost of living, Births, Deaths, Sporting events,
Book publications, Movies, Music, World events and People in power.

INDEX

UK EVENTS OF 1952

January

5th | Prime Minister Winston Churchill arrives in the United States for an official visit and talks with President Harry S. Truman.

10th | An Aer Lingus Douglas DC-3 aircraft on a London–Dublin flight crashes in Wales due to vertical draft in the mountains of Snowdonia, killing twenty passengers and the 3 crew.

16th | Sooty, Harry Corbett's glove puppet bear, first appears on BBC Television. The Sooty show didn't hit the screen until 1955.

22nd | First broadcast of The Goon Show under this title. Around the start of the third series at the end of the year, Spike Milligan, the principal writer, suffers a nervous breakdown. The first series, broadcast from 28th May to 20th September 1951, was titled Crazy People; subsequent series had the title The Goon Show from the 22nd January 1952.

30th | British troops remain in Korea, where they have spent the last eighteen months, after a breakdown of talks that were aimed at ending the Korean War.

February

1st | The first TV detector van is commissioned in the UK, as the beginning of a clampdown on the estimated 150,000 British households that watch television illegally without a licence. In 2013, the Radio Times obtained a leaked internal document from the BBC giving a breakdown of prosecutions for TV licence evasion. The 18-page document gave a breakdown of the number of people evading the charge, as well as mentioning the number of people employed to catch those who do not pay their television licence. However, no mention was made of TV detector vans being used to catch such people, prompting media speculation over the truth of their existence. In response a BBC spokeswoman rejected claims that the vans are a hoax: "Detector vans are an important part of our enforcement of the licence fee. We don't go into detail about how many there are or how they work as this information might be useful to people trying to evade the fee."

February

6th   King George VI dies at Sandringham House aged 56. It is revealed that he had been suffering from lung cancer. He is succeeded by his 25-year-old daughter, Princess Elizabeth, Duchess of Edinburgh, who ascends to the throne as Queen Elizabeth II. The new Queen is on a visit to Kenya at the time of her father's death and returns to London the following day. Known as "Bertie" among his family and close friends, George VI was born in the reign of his great-grandmother Queen Victoria and was named after his great-grandfather Albert, Prince Consort. As the second son of King George V, he was not expected to inherit the throne and spent his early life in the shadow of his elder brother, Edward. He attended naval college as a teenager and served in the Royal Navy and Royal Air Force during the First World War. In 1920, he was made Duke of York. He married Lady Elizabeth Bowes-Lyon in 1923, and they had two daughters, Elizabeth and Margaret. In the mid-1920s, he had speech therapy for a stammer, which he learned to manage to some degree. George's elder brother ascended the throne as Edward VIII after their father died in 1936. Later that year, Edward abdicated to marry the American socialite Wallis Simpson, and George became the third monarch of the House of Windsor.

8th   Queen Elizabeth II proclaimed Queen of the United Kingdom of Great Britain and Northern Ireland at St James's Palace.

14th   Great Britain and Northern Ireland compete at the Winter Olympics in Oslo and win one gold medal.

15th   From the 9th February for two days George VI's coffin rested in St Mary Magdalene Church, Sandringham, before lying in state at Westminster Hall from the 11th February. His funeral took place at St George's Chapel, Windsor Castle, on the 15th. He was interred initially in the Royal Vault until he was transferred to the King George VI Memorial Chapel inside St George's on the 26th March 1969. In 2002, fifty years after his death, the remains of his widow, Queen Elizabeth The Queen Mother, and the ashes of his younger daughter Princess Margaret, who both died that year, were interred in the chapel alongside him.

February

21st | On the 21st February 1952, it no longer became necessary to carry an identity card. The National Registration Act of 1939 was repealed on 22nd May 1952. The last person prosecuted under the Act was Harry Willcock. Even after the National Registration system was abandoned in 1952, the National Registration number persisted, being used within the National Health Service, for voter registration, and for the National Insurance System.

26th | Prime Minister Winston Churchill announces that the United Kingdom has an atomic bomb.

March

14th | BBC One Scotland is a British free-to-air television channel operated by BBC Scotland. It is the Scottish variation of the UK-wide BBC One. For all of the time the channel is referred to on screen as BBC One Scotland, sometimes using overlays to replace the normal channel identifier. The station also has its own team of continuity announcers, provided by BBC Scotland, to accommodate for the variations seen in Scotland from the rest of the BBC One network, whilst also providing the channel with an added Scottish identity. The announcers, based in Glasgow, also double up as transmission directors.

22nd | Wales wins Five Nations Rugby Championship; Grand Slam & Triple Crown with a 9-5 win over France at St. Helen's Ground, Swansea.

29th | The 98th Boat Race took place on the 29th March 1952. Held annually, the Boat Race is a side-by-side rowing race between crews from the Universities of Oxford and Cambridge along the River Thames. In a race umpired by former Cambridge rower Kenneth Payne, Oxford won by a canvas in a time of 20 minutes 23 seconds. At no point during the contest was there clear water between the boats. The race, described as "one of the closest fought of all time", was their second win in seven years and took the overall record in the event to 53–44 in Cambridge's favour.

31st | Computer scientist Alan Turing is convicted of "gross indecency" after admitting to a consensual homosexual relationship in Regina v. Turing and Murray. He consents to undergo oestrogen treatment to avoid imprisonment. Turing died in 1954, 16 days before his 42nd birthday, from cyanide poisoning. An inquest determined his death as a suicide, but it has been noted that the known evidence is also consistent with accidental poisoning.

In 2009, following an Internet campaign, British Prime Minister Gordon Brown made an official public apology on behalf of the British government for "the appalling way he was treated". Queen Elizabeth II granted Turing a posthumous pardon in 2013. The "Alan Turing law" is now an informal term for a 2017 law in the United Kingdom that retroactively pardoned man cautioned or convicted under historical legislation that outlawed homosexual acts.

April

5th | The 1952 Grand National was the 106th renewal of the Grand National horse race that took place at Aintree Racecourse near Liverpool, England, on the 5th April 1952. The race went off ten minutes late, after the field breached the starting tape, prompting a false start. It was won by Teal, a 100/7 shot ridden by jockey Arthur Thompson and trained by Neville Crump. Thompson and Crump were victorious in the steeplechase in 1948 also, with Sheila's Cottage, at odds of 50/1.

April

29th | On the 29th April 1952, the University of Southampton was granted full university status, allowing it to award its own degrees. The University of Southampton currently has 15,790 undergraduate and 6,925 postgraduate students, making it the largest university by higher education students in the South East region. The University of Southampton Students' Union provides support, representation and social activities for the students ranging from involvement in the Union's four media outlets, to any of the 200 affiliated societies and 80 sports. The university owns and operates a sports ground for use by students and also operates a sports centre on the main campus.

May

2nd | BOAC introduces the de Havilland DH.106 Comet 1 on its multi-stop London, England-Johannesburg, South Africa route, the first regular service flown by a jet airliner. G-ALYP makes the first flight, carrying 36 passengers.

3rd | A British Overseas Airways Corporation (BOAC) de Havilland Comet becomes the first jet airliner to arrive in South Africa, landing at Palmietfontein after a 24-hour journey with five refuelling stops en route.

12th | Squadron Leader P. G. Fisher makes the first non-stop, unrefuelled flight from England to Australia in an English Electric Canberra bomber in a record 23 hours 5 minutes.

15th | The Royal Air Force takes delivery of its last Avro Anson. The Anson had been in production for the RAF since 1934.

21st | The Eastcastle Street robbery was, at the time, Britain's largest post-war robbery. It occurred on Wednesday 21st May 1952 in Eastcastle Street when seven masked men held up a post office van just off Oxford Street, central London. The robbers escaped with £287,000 (estimated to be worth, in 2019, approximately £8,320,000). The robbers used two cars to sandwich the van. The first car emerged slowly from a side street causing the van to slow down, the second car then pulled up alongside. The driver and two attendants were dragged out and coshed and the van was stolen. It was later found abandoned near Regent's Park; 18 of the 31 mailbags were missing. It was found that the van's alarm bell had been tampered with. The robbery heralded the start of the 'project' crime. The mastermind behind the raid was London gangster Billy Hill and the robbers included George "Taters" Chatham and Terry "Lucky Tel" Hogan. Prime Minister Winston Churchill demanded daily updates on the police investigation and the Postmaster General, Earl de la Warr, was required to report to the Parliament of the United Kingdom on what had gone wrong. Yet, despite the involvement of over 1,000 police officers, no one was ever caught.

June

1st | One shilling charge is introduced for prescription drugs dispensed under the National Health Service.

2nd | Reindeer reintroduced to the Cairngorms of Scotland.

3rd | The last two miles of the Black Devon river disappear into old coal mine workings.

7th | Curtis Cup Women's Golf, Muirfield, Scotland: Great Britain & Ireland score first ever win in the contest; beat US, 5-4.

11th | Len Hutton became the first professional cricketer to captain England on this day – by coincidence, exactly a year after another legendary player, Dennis Compton, hit his 100th century. Over the decades and centuries its popularity grew, particularly among England's expensive schools and universities. A game at the newly opened Lord's in 1788 was listed as "Gentlemen Educated at Eton versus The Rest of the Schools". Over the decades and centuries its popularity grew, particularly among England's expensive schools and universities. A game at the newly opened Lord's in 1788 was listed as "Gentlemen Educated at Eton versus The Rest of the Schools".

July

5th | Six miners are killed in a mining accident at Point of Ayr colliery in north Wales.

6th | The last of the original trams runs in London; the citizens of London turn out in force to say farewell. "Operation Tramaway", the replacement of the tram service by diesel buses, was announced in July 1950 by Lord Latham of the London Transport Executive. Retirement started in October 1950 and London's final first-generation trams ran in the early hours of 6 July 1952 to a rousing reception at New Cross Depot.

19th | Great Britain and Northern Ireland compete at the Olympics in Helsinki and win 1 gold, 2 silver and 8 bronze medals.

20th | Arrow to the Heart is a British television drama, broadcast live twice by BBC Television in 1952, four days apart, and again in 1956. It was adapted from the 1950 German novel Unruhige Nacht by Albrecht Goes.

It was the first collaboration between director Rudolph Cartier and writer Nigel Kneale, who were both, according to television historian Lez Cooke, "responsible for introducing a completely new dimension to television drama in the early to mid-1950s."

August

6th | The Binnian Tunnel (2.5 miles long) was constructed between 1947 and 1950/51 and is located under the Mourne Mountains in County Down, Northern Ireland. The main purpose of the tunnel is to divert water from the Annalong Valley to the Silent Valley Reservoir underneath a number of mountains including Slieve Binnian, after which the tunnel was named. A high degree of engineering skills were employed in the building of the tunnel. A workforce of 150 was involved in two tunnelling teams which started from opposite ends and met in the middle nearly 800m under the roof of the mountain. The tunnel was created using drilling and blasting techniques. The shelters for the workers can be found on Slievenaglogh.
The tunnel was designed to carry 90 million imperial gallons (410,000 m3) of water per day, be 2.5 miles (4.0 km) long, 7 feet (2.1 m) high and 8 feet (2.4 m) wide. When the two teams met in the middle on 6 December 1950, they were only two inches out. The tunnel was officially opened on the 6th August 1952.

15th | Wenvoe transmitting station begins broadcasting 405-line VHF BBC Television to south Wales and the west of England on Band I channel 5 (66.75 MHz).

On the 15th and 16th of August 1952, a storm of tropical intensity broke over south-west England, depositing 229 millimetres (9.0 in) of rain within 24 hours on the already saturated soil of Exmoor, Devon. It is thought that a cold front scooped up a thunderstorm, and the orographic effect worsened the storm. Debris-laden floodwaters cascaded down the northern escarpment of the moor, converging upon the village of Lynmouth; in particular, in the upper West Lyn valley, fallen trees and other debris formed a dam, which in due course gave way, sending a huge wave of water and debris down the river. Overnight, more than 100 buildings were destroyed or seriously damaged along with 28 of the 31 bridges and 38 cars were washed out to sea. In total, 34 people died, with a further 420 made homeless. The seawall and Rhenish Tower survived the main flood, but were seriously undermined. The tower collapsed into the river the next day, causing a temporary flood.

26th | Hit radio series Welsh Rarebit, broadcast from the BBC Cardiff studios, transfers to television.

September

3rd | Mahmood Hussein Mattan is the last person to be executed at Cardiff Prison.

6th | On the 6th September 1952, a prototype de Havilland DH.110 jet fighter crashed during an aerial display at the Farnborough Air show in Hampshire, England. The jet disintegrated mid-air during an aerobatic manoeuvre, causing the death of pilot John Derry and on-board flight test observer Anthony Richards. Debris from the aircraft fell onto a crowd of spectators, killing 29 people and injuring 60. The cause of the break-up was later determined to be structural failure due to a design flaw in the wing's leading edge. All DH.110s were initially grounded, but after modification to its design, the type entered service with the Royal Navy as the Sea Vixen.

19th | English film star Charlie Chaplin, sailing to the United Kingdom with his family for the premiere of his film Limelight (London, 16th October), is told that he will be refused re-entry to the United States until he has been investigated by the U.S. Immigration Service. He chooses to remain in Europe.

27th | The Commando Memorial is a Category A listed monument in Lochaber, Scotland, dedicated to the men of the original British Commando Forces raised during World War II. Situated around a mile from Spean Bridge, it overlooks the training areas of the Commando Training Depot established in 1942 at Achnacarry Castle. Unveiled by the Queen Mother, it is one of Scotland's best-known monuments, both as a war memorial and as a tourist attraction offering views of Ben Nevis and Aonach Mòr.

September

29th | John Rhodes Cobb was an early to mid-20th Century English racing motorist. He was three times holder of the World Land Speed Record, in 1938, 1939 and 1947, set at Bonneville Speedway in Utah, US. He was awarded the Segrave Trophy in 1947. He was killed in 1952 whilst piloting a jet powered speedboat attempting to break the World Water Speed Record on Loch Ness water in Scotland.

October

3rd | Operation Hurricane was the first test of a British atomic device. A plutonium implosion device was detonated on the 3rd October 1952 in the lagoon in the Monte Bello Islands in Western Australia. With the success of Operation Hurricane, Britain became the third nuclear power after the United States and the Soviet Union.

5th | Tea rationing ends, after thirteen years, as announced by the Government two days earlier.

8th | The Harrow and Wealdstone rail crash was a three-train collision at Harrow and Wealdstone station in Wealdstone, Middlesex (now Greater London) during the morning rush hour of 8 October 1952. 112 were killed and 340 injured, 88 of these being detained in hospital and it remains the worst peacetime rail crash in the United Kingdom.

19th | A small Welsh republican group, Y Gweriniaethwyr, make an unsuccessful attempt to blow up a water pipeline leading from the Claerwen dam in mid Wales to Birmingham. The Claerwen reservoir is officially opened on the 23rd October.

November

1st | Royal College of General Practitioners established. The RCGP represents and supports GPs on key issues including licensing, education, training, research and clinical standards. It is the largest of the medical royal colleges, with over 50,000 members. The RCGP was founded in 1952 in London, England and is a registered charity.

November

12th Murder of Patricia Curran, 19-year-old daughter of Sir Lancelot Curran. Iain Hay Gordon was found guilty of her murder, but the sentence was overturned in 2000.

14th The magazine New Musical Express publishes the first UK Singles Chart.

25th On the 25th November 1952, 453 people took their seats in the Ambassadors Theatre for the London premiere of Christie's "Mousetrap." The drama is played out at "Monkswell Manor," whose hosts and guests are snowed in among radio reports of a murderer on the loose.

29th "Pillar Box War": First GPO pillar box of the present reign to be erected in Scotland, on the Inch housing estate in Edinburgh, is attacked in protest at its bearing the Royal Cipher of Elizabeth II, the regnal number being considered historically incorrect in Scotland.

December

5th Ness, Lewis, selected for influenza vaccine trials.

10th Archer Martin and Richard Synge win the Nobel Prize in Chemistry "for their invention of partition chromatography".

Caithness Education Committee rejects a plan to issue pupils with a book entitled ABC Guide to the Coronation because it contains only English history.

18th Flower Pot Men was a British children's programme, produced by BBC television, first transmitted in 1952, and repeated regularly for more than twenty years. A reboot of the show called Bill and Ben was produced in 2001.

25th The Queen makes her first Christmas speech to the Commonwealth.

Look inside —

then compare!

SEE WHY DU MONTS DO MORE

You need not be an expert to see for yourself the reason for Du Mont's outstanding performance. This is television's most precise instrument, built with more tubes, extra-size parts, and a solid, orderly design that reflects expert engineering and painstaking craftsmanship. Look at the Du Mont chassis. Compare it with others. Then you will know why owning a Du Mont is full assurance of long years of satisfaction.

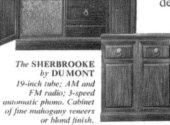

The SHERBROOKE by DU MONT 19-inch tube; AM and FM radio; 3-speed automatic phono. Cabinet of fine mahogany veneers or blond finish. Styled by Herbert Rosengren.

DU MONT

First with the finest in Television

Lucozade

the sparkling GLUCOSE *drink*

TIME FOR LUCOZADE!

In hot summer days when your energy flags and you feel ' all in '—then is the time for delicious Lucozade! This sparkling drink contains Glucose, nature's great energiser, in the most delicious form imaginable. It is instantly refreshing, wonderfully sustaining. Lucozade replaces your vitality *quickly* and *pleasantly*. Keep a supply handy—and drink Lucozade regularly!

2/6d. plus 3d. bottle deposit (returnable). Also in handy size at 8d. plus 2d. bottle deposit.

Lucozade is used by Doctors and Nurses in Clinics, Hospitals and Nursing Homes.

Lucozade *REFRESHES AND SUSTAINS*

LUCOZADE LTD., GREAT WEST ROAD, BRENTFORD, MIDDX.

royds

James Aloysius Hansom knew a <u>good</u> <u>thing</u>

In 1834 His Design for a "Patent Safety Cab" Sold for a Fortune!

James Hansom, of London, was a prominent Victorian architect—but his most distinctive contribution to the London scene was not a building but the familiar two-wheeled "hansom cab." This unique conveyance replaced almost all other public vehicles, and remained a common sight for nearly three-quarters of a century. Mr. Hansom's original design was briefly sketched out in 1834—and was promptly purchased by a coach maker for 10,000 pounds sterling!

If you know a <u>good</u> <u>thing</u> in whiskey...

you'll try HUNTER and discover why it will be *your* whiskey ever afterwards. For Hunter is light enough for you to sip it straight yet hearty enough to hold its own in a highball.

Today's great blend for *today's* good tastes. Why not *try* Hunter!

Hunter-Wilson Distilling Co., Inc., Louisville, Ky. Blended Whiskey 86.8 Proof. 65% grain neutral spirits.

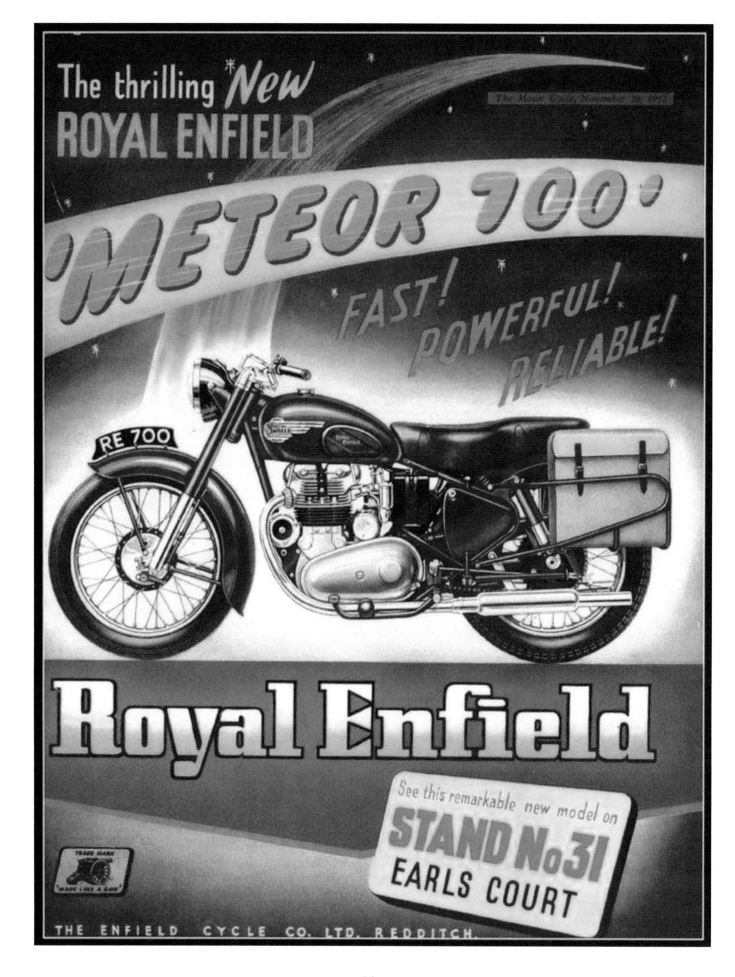

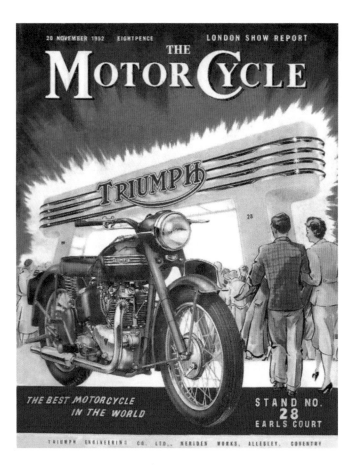

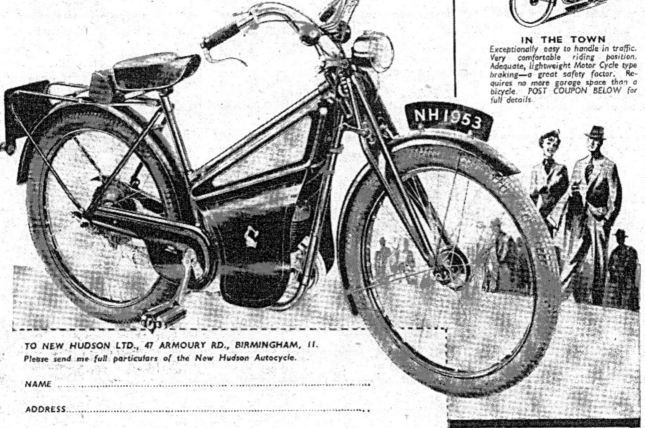

COST OF LIVING 1952

A conversion of pre-decimal to decimal money

The Pound, 1971 became the year of decimalization when the pound became 100 new pennies. Prior to that the pound was equivalent to 20 shillings. Money prior to 1971 was written £/s/d. (d being for pence). Below is a chart explaining the monetary value of each coin before and after 1971.

Symbol	Before 1971	After 1971
£	Pound (240 pennies)	Pound (100 new pennies)
s	Shilling (12 pennies)	5 pence
d	Penny	¼ of a penny
¼d	Farthing	1 penny
½d	Halfpenny	½ pence
3d	Threepence	About 1/80 of a pound
4d	Groat (four pennies)	
6d	Sixpence (Tanner)	2½ new pence
2s	Florin (2 shillings)	10 pence
2s/6d	Half a crown (2 shillings and 6 pence)	12½ pence
5s	Crown	25 pence
10s	10 shilling note (10 bob)	50 pence
10s/6d	½ Guinea	52½ pence
21s	1 Guinea	105 pence

Prices are in equivalent to new pence today and on average throughout the UK.

Item	1952	Price equivalent in today's money
Wages, average yearly	£375.00	£10,650.00
Average house price	£1,891.00	£53,704.00
Price of an average car	£620.00	£17,608.00
Litre of petrol	£0.05p	£1.33p
Flour 1.5kg	£0.08p	£2.19p
Bread (loaf)	£0.03p	£0.88p
Sugar 1kg	£0.06p	£1.82p
Milk 1 pint	£0.11p	£3.07p
Butter 250g	£0.08p	£2.36p
Cheese 400g	£0.10p	£2.72p
Potatoes 2.5kg	£0.04p	£1.28p
Bacon 400g	£0.18p	£5.20p
Beer (Pint)	£0.06p	£1.82p

Prices are an average throughout the United Kingdom and not per city.

Telephone calls

Only 14% of households had a telephone in 1952.

The cost of installing a telephone was £5. You paid a quarterly rental of £3.

The rental charge included 100 free calls per year. Telephone calls were charged on a different basis from today. There were two types of call 'local' or 'trunk' calls. Local calls were within the local exchange area.

Local calls

For local calls it didn't matter how long you were on the phone as the charge was for a single call. In spite of this people used the telephone for short functional calls. Most took less than two minutes. Charges for local calls in 1956 were:

Distance	Cost	in today's money
Up to 5 miles	2d	15p
5 to 7½ miles	4d	29p
7½ to 12½ miles	6d	44p
12½ to 15 miles	8d	58p

Trunk calls

For a Trunk call you needed to contact the operator and ask her (it was usually a her) to dial the number for you. Trunk calls were charged per 3 minute duration. The operator worked out the charge. There was a cheap rate period from 6pm to 10.30pm every day.

Posting letters

At the beginning of the 1950s, it cost just 2½d (1p) to post a letter in the UK. The GPO (General Post Office) increased the cost to 3d in 1957.

Sending a postcard home from your holidays was cheaper. It cost 2d before 1957, then 2½d

Television

Televisions were expensive in the 1950s and you could only view programmes in black and white. There was also just one BBC channel. Commercial TV started in 1955, so viewers had a choice of two channels. Most deserted the BBC for ITV.

In 1951 a Murphy V200 television with a 12" screen cost £80 [£1800 in today's money].

At the end of the decade a 17" Murphy set cost £69 16s 6d [£1100 in today's money].

In that time television ownership increased from a tiny fraction of the population to around three quarters of all households.

Ball point pens were new in 1945. At the beginning of the 1950s they were still relatively expensive, but prices came down quickly.

Platinum ballpoint - 1950 - 5s (£6 in today's money)

Groceries

People bought a lot of canned and tinned produce in the 1950s. It was a trend that began in the 1930s. They had also developed a taste for breakfast cereals and instant coffee.

These are some typical groceries people bought in the 1950s and the approximate prices.

Canned/bottled meat and fish
Maconochie's steak pudding - 16oz - 1s 10d
Chef herring in tomato - 14oz - 1s 7d
Heinz fish and meat pastes - medium size - 1s 2d

Canned fruit and fruit juices
Smedley's rhubarb - size A2 - 1s 1½d
Smedley's golden plum - size A2½ - 1s 5½d
Anderson, Richards Sunkist Californian pure lemon juice - 6oz - 9d

Canned vegetables
Crosse & Blackwell beans in tomato - per tin - 10d
Smedley baked beans - per tin - 10d
Heinz baked beans in tomato - 5oz - 5½d
Heinz spaghetti in tomato with cheese - 16oz - 10½d
Bachelor's garden peas - A1 - 1s 1d
Bachelor's processed peas (dwarf) - A1 - 6d

Soups
Heinz tomato - 15½oz - 1s 1½d
Crosse & Blackwell cream of vegetable - tin - 1s
Sauces and pickles

These are some classic sauces. You can still buy most of them today.

HP sauce - 7oz - 10½d
Daddies sauce - 7oz - 10½d
Chef tomato ketchup - medium - 1s
G Mason OK sauce - 9oz - 1s 4½d
Maconchies's Pan Yan pickle - 11oz - 1s 5d
Crosse & Blackwell Branston pickle - 11½oz - 1s 4½d
Colman's mustard - 4oz - 1s 4½d
Heinz Salad Cream - medium - 1s 4½d

Hot drinks
Nescafé instant coffee - medium - 2s 9d
Lyons Chico [instant coffee with chicory and glucose] -¼lb - 2s 4d
Lyons Bev [liquid coffee similar to Camp] - family size - 2s 1½d
Maxwell House instant coffee - 2oz - 2s 8d
Cadbury's Bourne-Vita - ½lb - 2s 9d
Brooke Bond PG Tips tea - 1lb - 6s 8d

BRITISH BIRTHS

Timothy Malcolm Healy was born on the 29th January 1952 and is an English actor. Timothy Malcolm Healy was born in the Benwell area of Newcastle upon Tyne. He worked as a welder in a factory and joined the British Army, serving part-time in the 4th Battalion, Parachute Regiment. In 1983, Healy was brought to public attention for his role in Auf Wiedersehen, Pet a TV comedy drama series about British builders working in Germany. When Healy's wife, Denise Welch, was a guest on The Paul O'Grady Show, an apparently aged man came on the show to talk about a subject. He sounded unwell while Welch was speaking, and to her and everyone's surprise, he revealed himself to be Healy. Healy starred in the third series of the ITV comedy Benidorm playing a cross dresser called Lesley. He later became a regular in the fourth series in 2011. His character is really called Les and has a son, Liam. Healy has also had a role in Vic Reeves and Bob Mortimer's show Catterick as a helpful man with a chronically cold wife.

William Joseph Dunlop OBE was born on the 25th February 1952 and sadly passed away on the 2nd July 2000. He was a Northern Irish motorcyclist from Ballymoney. He won his third hat trick at the Isle of Man TT in 2000 and set his fastest lap on the course of 123.87 mph in the Senior race, which he finished third. The bend at 26th milestone on the Isle of Man was named in his honour. In 2016 he was voted through Motorcycle News as the fifth greatest motorcycling icon ever, behind Valentino Rossi. During his career he won the Ulster Grand Prix 24 times. In 1986, he won a fifth consecutive TT Formula One world title; initially based on one race at the Isle of Man TT after the loss of World Championship status from 1977-onwards and organised by the Auto-Cycle Union, the title was eventually expanded to take in more rounds in other countries. He was awarded the MBE in 1986 for his services to the sport, and in 1996 he was awarded the OBE for his humanitarian work for children in Romanian orphanages, to which he had delivered clothing and food.

General David Julian Richards, Baron Richards of Herstmonceux, GCB, CBE, DSO, DL was born on the 4th March 1952 is a retired senior British Army officer who was formerly the Chief of the Defence Staff, the professional head of the British Armed Forces. David Richards served in the Far East, Germany and Northern Ireland with the Royal Artillery before commanding forces in East Timor and most notably Sierra Leone, where his action without official sanctioning protected Freetown from rebel attacks during the Sierra Leone Civil War. Richards became Commander-in-Chief, Land Forces of the British Army in 2008 and held this role until 2009 when he was appointed Chief of the General Staff, the head of the British Army. He was appointed as Chief of the Defence Staff the following year. He was succeeded by General Sir Nicholas Houghton on the 18th July 2013. In 2014, Richards was created a Life Peer taking the title Baron Richards of Herstmonceux. He sits in the House of Lords as a crossbencher.

Douglas Noel Adams was born on the 11th March 1952 and passed away on the 11th May 2001. He was an English author, screenwriter, essayist, humourist, satirist and dramatist. Douglas Adams was author of The Hitchhiker's Guide to the Galaxy, which originated in 1978 as a BBC radio comedy before developing into a "trilogy" of five books that sold more than 15 million copies in his lifetime and generated a television series, several stage plays, comics, a video game, and in 2005 a feature film. Adams's contribution to UK radio is commemorated in The Radio Academy's Hall of Fame. Adams also wrote Dirk Gently's Holistic Detective Agency (1987) and The Long Dark Tea-Time of the Soul (1988), and co-wrote The Meaning of Liff (1983), The Deeper Meaning of Liff (1990), and Last Chance to See (1990). He wrote two stories for the television series Doctor Who, co-wrote City of Death, and served as script editor for its seventeenth season in 1979. He co-wrote the Monty Python sketch "Patient Abuse" which appeared in the final episode of Monty Python's Flying Circus.

Anthony William Brise born 28th March 1952 and died 29th November 1975. He was an English racing driver, who took part in ten Formula One Grand Prix events in 1975, before dying in a plane crash with Graham Hill. Tony Brise won his first UK championship in 1969, and switched to single-seater racing. In 1971 he placed second in the BOC British FF1600 Championship. Brise made his Grand Prix debut on the 27th April 1975 for Williams at the Spanish Grand Prix in Montjuic Park near Barcelona, a controversial race marred by strikes over safety issues, a high number of crashes, and the deaths of four spectators. Brise finished seventh in this race, two laps behind the leaders. On 29 November 1975, Hill and Brise, along with Andy Smallman, the team's designer, and three team mechanics, were returning to London from southern France, where they were testing a new race car, the GH2. The Embassy Hill plane, a twin-engine six-seat Piper Aztec piloted by Hill, was attempting to land at Elstree Airfield at night in thick fog when it crashed and burned at Arkley golf course, killing all six aboard. Tony Brise was 23 years old.

Allan Wipper Wells MBE was born on the 3rd May 1952and is a former British track and field sprinter who became the 100 metres Olympic champion at the 1980 Summer Olympics in Moscow. Within a fortnight of that, he also took on and beat America's best sprinters at an invitational meeting in Koblenz. In 1981, Wells was both the IAAF Golden Sprints and IAAF World Cup gold medallist. He is also a three-time European Cup gold medallist among many other sprint successes. He was a multiple medallist for his native Scotland at the Commonwealth Games, winning two golds at the 1978 Commonwealth Games and completing a 100 metres/200 metres sprint double at the 1982 Commonwealth Games. Wells also recorded the fastest British 100/200 times in 1978, 1979, 1980, 1981, 1982, 1983 and 100 m in 1984. He began concentrating on sprint events in 1976. In 1977 he won the AAA's Indoor 60 metres title, and won his first of seven outdoor Scottish sprint titles. In the 1978 season his times and victories continued to improve, he clocked a new British record at Gateshead 10.29, beating Don Quarrie and James Sanford.

William John Neeson OBE was born on the 7th June 1952 and is an actor from Northern Ireland. He got his first film experience in 1977, playing Jesus Christ and Evangelist in the religious film Pilgrim's Progress (1978). In 1980, filmmaker John Boorman saw him on stage as Lennie Small in Of Mice and Men and offered him the role of Sir Gawain in the Arthurian film Excalibur. Steven Spielberg offered Neeson the role of Oskar Schindler in his holocaust film, Schindler's List, after seeing him in Anna Christie on Broadway. Kevin Costner, Mel Gibson and Warren Beatty all expressed interest in portraying Schindler, but Neeson was cast in December 1992 after formally auditioning for the role. His critically acclaimed performance earned him a nomination for a Best Actor Oscar, and helped the film earn Best Picture of 1993. In 1999, Neeson starred as Jedi Master Qui-Gon Jinn in Star Wars: Episode I – The Phantom Menace. Director George Lucas cast Neeson in the role because he considered him a "master actor, who the other actors will look up to, who has got the qualities of strength that the character demands."

Estelle Morris, Baroness Morris of Yardley, PC was born on the 17th June 1952 and is a British Labour Party politician, who was the Member of Parliament (MP) for Birmingham Yardley from 1992 to 2005, and served briefly in the Cabinet as Secretary of State for Education and Skills from 2001 to 2002. Estelle Morris was elected to Parliament in 1992 for Birmingham Yardley, gaining the seat from the Conservatives with a majority of only 162. She became a minister in the Department for Education and Employment in 1997 and was promoted to Secretary of State for Education and Skills in 2001. She suddenly resigned her post in October 2002, explaining that she did not feel up to the job. She re-joined the Government in 2003 as Minister for the Arts in the Department for Culture, Media and Sport, and caused further comment when she admitted that she did not know much about contemporary art. She stepped down from the government and as a Member of Parliament at the 2005 general election. Morris is the Chair of the medical charity, APS Support UK, for Antiphospholipid syndrome.

John Graham Kettley was born on the 11th July 1952 in Halifax, West Yorkshire and is an English freelance weatherman. He worked at the meteorological office at Manchester Airport for two years from 1970 before studying applied health and social care at what is now Coventry University, where he met his wife. He spent four years researching meteorology. He trained for a year in weather presentation at the Met Office College, Shinfeild near Reading. From 1980, he worked at the Nottingham Weather Centre, presenting his first forecast for Radio Lincolnshire, then further forecasts for Midlands Today and Central Television. In 1985, he became a national forecaster on the BBC. In 2000 John Kettley left the Met Office to join commercial weather company British Weather Services, and continues to provide forecasts across a range of media outlets and sporting concerns including the Football Association, Twickenham and leading UK racecourses such as Newbury, Cheltenham, Haydock Park, Newmarket and Barbecues. John Kettley enjoys playing cricket, fell-walking and horse racing.

Alexei David Sayle was born on the 7th August 1952 is an English stand-up comedian, actor, television presenter, author and former recording artist, and was a central figure in the British alternative comedy movement in the 1980s. When the Comedy Store opened in London in 1979, Sayle responded to an advert in Private Eye for would-be comedians and became its first master of ceremonies. He appeared on The Comic Strip Album (1981) and recorded Cak! (1982). He also appeared in the stage show, film and comedy album of The Secret Policeman's Other Ball. He played various roles in the situation comedy The Young Ones (1982–1984), along with Adrian Edmondson, Rik Mayall, Nigel Planer and Christopher Ryan. Sayle was signed in 1992 to a seven-year contract to play an Eastern European chef as a regular character on the American sitcom The Golden Palace, the sequel to The Golden Girls, but was fired and replaced by Cheech Marin before the pilot was shot. He appeared in the 1992 Carry On film, Carry On Columbus. Sayle has released five comedy singles. His most successful single was "'Ullo John! Gotta New Motor?"

John Graham Mellor born 21st August 1952 and passed away on the 22nd December 2002. He is better known as Joe Strummer, was a British musician, singer, songwriter, composer, actor, and radio host who were best known as the co-founder, lyricist, rhythm guitarist, and co-lead vocalist of punk rock band The Clash. Formed in 1976, the Clash's second album Give 'Em Enough Rope (1978) reached No. 2 on the UK charts. Soon after, they achieved success in the US, starting with London Calling (1979) and peaking with Combat Rock (1982), which reached No. 7 on the US charts and was certified 2× platinum there. The Clash's explosive political lyrics, musical experimentation, and rebellious attitude had a far-reaching influence on rock music in general, especially alternative rock. Their music incorporated reggae, ska, dub, funk, rap and rockabilly. Strummer's other career highlights included stints with the 101ers, Latino Rockabilly War, the Mescalero's, and the Pogues, as well as solo music. Strummer and the Clash were inducted into the Rock and Roll Hall of Fame in January 2003.

Jack Wild born 30th September 1952 and died on the 1st March 2006. He was an English actor and singer, best known for his debut role as the Artful Dodger in Oliver! (1968), for which he received an Academy Award nomination for Best Supporting Actor as well as Golden Globe and BAFTA nominations. In the spring of 1966, Wild left the stage show of Oliver! To make the film serial Danny the Dragon for the Children's Film Foundation. Wild's first speaking roles on TV were in an episode of Out of the Unknown, and in the third part of the BBC's version of the 'Wesker trilogy', I'm Talking About Jerusalem. He also appeared in episodes of Z-Cars, The Newcomers and George and the Dragon. By 1973, aged 21, he was an alcoholic. After exhausting his remaining fortune, Wild lived with his retired father for a few years. Jack Wild eventually became sober on the 6th March 1989, after joining the support group, Alcoholics Victorious. He returned to the big screen in a few minor roles, such as in the 1991 Kevin Costner film Robin Hood: Prince of Thieves and as a peddler in Basil (1998). Wild died just before midnight on the 1st March 2006, following a long battle with cancer.

Melvyn Kenneth Smith born 3rd December 1952 and passed away on the 19th July 2013. He was an English comedian and film director. John Lloyd later got the opportunity to develop the idea that became the satirical BBC television series Not the Nine O'clock News. This was followed briefly by Smith and Goody (with Bob Goody) and then the comedy sketch series Alas Smith and Jones, co-starring Griff Rhys Jones. In 1981, Smith and Griff Rhys Jones founded TalkBack Productions, a company that has produced many of the most significant British comedy shows of the past two decades, including Smack the Pony, Da Ali G Show; I'm Alan Partridge and Big Train. In 2000, the company was sold to Pearson for £62 million. In 1987, Smith recorded a single with Kim Wilde for Comic Relief: a cover of the Christmas song Rockin' Around the Christmas Tree with some additional comedy lines written by Smith and Jones. On the morning of the 19th July 2013, the London Ambulance Service was called to Smith's home in north-west London. Smith was confirmed dead by the ambulance crew, with a later post-mortem confirming death from a heart attack.

Clive Stuart Anderson was born on the 10th December 1952 and is an English television and radio presenter, comedy writer and former barrister. Anderson was involved in the fledgling alternative comedy scene in the early 1980s and was the first act to come on stage at The Comedy Store when it opened in 1979. He made his name as host of the improvised television comedy show Whose Line Is It Anyway? which ran for 10 series. Anderson hosted his own chat show, Clive Anderson Talks Back (1989–1996), on Channel 4, which ran for 10 series. He has made ten appearances on Have I Got News for You. He has also frequently appeared on QI. In 2007, he featured as a regular panellist on the ITV comedy show News Knight. Clive presents the legal show Unreliable Evidence on Radio 4. He also covered the Sunday morning 11 a.m. to 1 p.m. show on BBC Radio 2 through the end of January 2008. Anderson is a comedy sketch writer who has written for Frankie Howerd, Not the Nine O'clock News, and Griff Rhys Jones and Mel Smith.

Jennifer Ann Agutter OBE was born on the 20th December 1952 she is a British actress. She began her career as a child actress in 1964, appearing in East of Sudan, Star! and two adaptations of The Railway Children—the BBC's 1968 television serial and the 1970 film version. She relocated to the United States in 1974 to pursue a Hollywood career and subsequently appeared in Logan's Run (1976), Amy (1981), An American Werewolf in London (1981) to name but a few. After returning to Britain in the early 1990s to pursue family life, Agutter shifted her focus to television, and in 2000, she appeared in a new television adaptation of The Railway Children, this time taking on the role of the mother. She has continued to work steadily in British television drama, and since 2012, she has starred in the BBC's primetime ratings hit Call the Midwife. She also made a return to Hollywood film-making in 2012, appearing in Marvel's The Avengers, and reprised her role in Captain America: The Winter Soldier (2014). She supports several charitable causes, mostly in relation to cystic fibrosis.

BRITISH DEATHS

George VI Albert Frederick Arthur George was born on the 14th December 1895 and sadly passed away on the 6th February 1952 and was King of the United Kingdom and the Dominions of the British Commonwealth from the 11th December 1936 until his death. He was concurrently the last emperor of India until August 1947, when the British Raj was dissolved. Known as "Bertie" among his family and close friends, George VI was born in the reign of his great-grandmother Queen Victoria and was named after his great-grandfather Albert, Prince Consort. In 1920, he was made Duke of York. He married Lady Elizabeth Bowes-Lyon in 1923, and they had two daughters, Elizabeth and Margaret. In the mid-1920s, he had speech therapy for a stammer, which he learned to manage to some degree. George's elder brother ascended the throne as Edward VIII after their father died in 1936. Later that year, Edward abdicated to marry the American socialite Wallis Simpson, and George became the third monarch of the House of Windsor.

John Rhodes Cobb was born on the 2nd December 1899 and died on the 29th September 1952 and was an early to mid-20th Century English racing motorist. In 1928 he privately purchased a 10.5-litre Delage which was imported to England from the factory in Paris, which he raced at Brooklands from 1929 to 1933, breaking the flying start outer lap Record three times in these years, and being clocked at a top speed of 138.88 miles per hour on 2 July 1932. In 1932 he also won the British Empire Trophy at Brooklands. In 1933 he privately commissioned the design and construction of the 24-litre "Napier Railton" from "Thomson & Taylor", with which he broke a number of track speed records, including setting the ultimate lap record at the Brooklands race track which was never surpassed, driving at an average speed of 143.44 mph. During World War II, he served as a pilot in the Royal Air Force, and between 1943 and 1945 served with the Air Transport Auxiliary.

Colonel Windham Henry Wyndham-Quin, 5th Earl of Dunraven and Mount-Earl CB DSO born 7th February 1857 and died on the 23rd October 1952. He was an Irish Peer, British Army officer and a Conservative Member of Parliament for South Glamorganshire. Wyndham-Quin was a major in the 16th Lancers, and served in the First Boer War in 1881. He again volunteered for service in South Africa in early 1900, during the Second Boer War, and was appointed a captain in the Imperial Yeomanry on 14 February 1900. He raised and commanded the 4th (Glamorgan) Company, IY, which left Liverpool on the SS Cymric in March 1900 to serve as a company of the 1st Battalion Imperial Yeomanry. On 18th April 1900 he was appointed 2nd in command of this battalion. He was mentioned in despatches, received the Queen's medal (3 clasps), and was awarded the Distinguished Service Order (DSO) in November 1900. On return from South Africa he raised and commanded the Glamorgan Imperial Yeomanry, a full regiment that perpetuated 4th Company.

SPORTING EVENTS 1952

1952 County Cricket Season

1952 was the 53rd season of County Championship cricket in England. It was the beginning of Surrey's period of dominance as they won the first of seven successive County Championships. The club's home ground is The Oval, in the Kennington area of Lambeth in South London. They have been based there continuously since 1845. The club also has an 'out ground' at Woodbridge Road, Guildford, where some home games are played each season. Surrey's long history includes three major periods of great success. The club was unofficially proclaimed as "Champion County" seven times during the 1850s; it won the title eight times in nine years from 1887 to 1895 (including the first official County Championship in 1890); and won seven consecutive titles from 1952 to 1958. Surrey won 23 of its 28 county matches in 1955, the most wins by any team in the County Championship and a record which can no longer be beaten. Surrey have won the County Championship 19 times outright (and shared once), a number exceeded only by Yorkshire, with their most recent win being in 2018.

Position	Team	Played	Won	Lost	Drawn	Tied	No Dec	1st inn lead match L	1st inn lead match D	Points
1	Surrey	28	20	3	5	0	0	0	4	256
2	Yorkshire	28	17	2	8	0	1	0	5	224
3	Lancashire	28	12	3	11	1	1	1	8	188
4	Derbyshire	28	11	8	9	0	0	2	6	164
5	Middlesex	28	11	12	4	0	1	0	1	136
6	Leicestershire	28	9	9	9	0	1	1	5	132
7	Glamorgan	28	8	7	13	0	0	2	6	130
8	Northamptonshire	28	7	8	12	0	1	3	8	128
9	Gloucestershire	28	7	10	11	0	0	4	6	124
=10	Essex	28	8	4	13	1	2	1	4	120
=10	Warwickshire	28	8	10	8	1	1	0	4	120
12	Hampshire	28	7	11	9	0	1	4	3	112
13	Sussex	28	7	12	6	1	2	0	2	96
14	Worcestershire	28	6	11	10	0	1	1	3	90
15	Kent	28	5	15	8	0	0	2	4	84
16	Nottinghamshire	28	3	11	13	0	1	2	7	72
17	Somerset	28	2	12	13	0	1	1	4	44

1951–52 in English football

After the title disappointments of the previous five seasons, Manchester United finally ended their 41-year wait for the First Division title, finishing four points ahead of their nearest rivals, Tottenham Hotspur and Arsenal. They then won back-to-back league titles in 1956 and 1957; the squad, who had an average age of 22, were nicknamed "the Busby Babes" by the media, a testament to Busby's faith in his youth players. In 1957, Manchester United became the first English team to compete in the European Cup, despite objections from The Football League, who had denied Chelsea the same opportunity the previous season.

Huddersfield Town and Fulham were relegated to the Second Division.

Pos	Team	Pld	HW	HD	HL	AW	AD	AL	Pts
1	Manchester United	42	15	3	3	8	8	5	57
2	Tottenham Hotspur	42	16	1	4	6	8	7	53
3	Arsenal	42	13	7	1	8	4	9	53
4	Portsmouth	42	13	3	5	7	5	9	48
5	Bolton Wanderers	42	11	7	3	8	3	10	48
6	Aston Villa	42	13	3	5	6	6	9	47
7	Preston North End	42	10	5	6	7	7	7	46
8	Newcastle United	42	12	4	5	6	5	10	45
9	Blackpool	42	12	5	4	6	4	11	45
10	Charlton Athletic	42	12	5	4	5	5	11	44
11	Liverpool	42	6	11	4	6	8	7	43
12	Sunderland	42	8	6	7	7	6	8	42
13	West Bromwich Albion	42	8	9	4	6	4	11	41
14	Burnley	42	9	6	6	6	4	11	40
15	Manchester City	42	7	5	9	6	8	7	39
16	Wolverhampton Wanderers	42	8	6	7	4	8	9	38
17	Derby County	42	10	4	7	5	3	13	37
18	Middlesbrough	42	12	4	5	3	2	16	36
19	Chelsea	42	10	3	8	4	5	12	36
20	Stoke City	42	8	6	7	4	1	16	31
21	Huddersfield Town	42	9	3	9	1	5	15	28
22	Fulham	42	5	7	9	3	4	14	27

1951–52 Scottish Division A

The 1951–52 Scottish Division A was won by Hibernian by four points over nearest rival Rangers. Greenock Morton and Stirling Albion finished 15th and 16th respectively and were relegated to the 1952–53 Scottish Division B.

Pos	Team	Pld	W	D	L	GF	GA	GD	Pts
1	Hibernian	30	20	5	5	92	36	+56	45
2	Rangers	30	16	9	5	61	31	+30	41
3	East Fife	30	17	3	10	71	49	+22	37
4	Heart of Midlothian	30	14	7	9	69	53	+16	35
5	Raith Rovers	30	14	5	11	43	42	+1	33
6	Partick Thistle	30	12	7	11	48	51	−3	31
7	Motherwell	30	12	7	11	51	57	−6	31
8	Dundee	30	11	6	13	53	52	+1	28
9	Celtic	30	10	8	12	52	55	−3	28
10	Queen of the South	30	10	8	12	50	60	−10	28
11	Aberdeen	30	10	7	13	65	58	+7	27
12	Third Lanark	30	9	8	13	51	62	−11	26
13	Airdrieonians	30	11	4	15	54	69	−15	26
14	St Mirren	30	10	5	15	43	58	−15	25
15	Morton	30	9	6	15	49	56	−7	24
16	Stirling Albion	30	5	5	20	36	99	−63	15

1951–52 Scottish Division B

The 1951–52 Scottish Division B was won by Clyde who, along with second placed Falkirk, were promoted to Division A. Arbroath finished bottom.

Pos	Team	Pld	W	D	L	GF	GA	GD	Pts
1	Clyde	30	19	6	5	100	45	+55	44
2	Falkirk	30	18	7	5	80	34	+46	43
3	Ayr United	30	17	5	8	55	45	+10	39
4	Dundee United	30	16	5	9	75	60	+15	37
5	Kilmarnock	30	16	2	12	62	48	+14	34
6	Dunfermline Athletic	30	15	2	13	74	65	+9	32
7	Alloa Athletic	30	13	6	11	55	49	+6	32
8	Cowdenbeath	30	12	8	10	66	67	−1	32
9	Hamilton Academical	30	12	6	12	47	51	−4	30
10	Dumbarton	30	10	8	12	51	57	−6	28
11	St Johnstone	30	9	7	14	62	68	−6	25
12	Forfar Athletic	30	10	4	16	59	97	−38	24
13	Stenhousemuir	30	8	6	16	57	74	−17	22
14	Albion Rovers	30	6	10	14	39	57	−18	22
15	Queen's Park	30	8	4	18	40	62	−22	20
16	Arbroath	30	6	4	20	40	83	−43	16

1952 Five Nations Championship

The 1952 Five Nations Championship was the twenty-third series of the rugby union Five Nations Championship. Including the previous incarnations as the Home Nations and Five Nations, this was the fifty-eighth series of the northern hemisphere rugby union championship. Ten matches were played between the 12th January and the 5th April. It was contested by England, France, Ireland, Scotland and Wales. Wales won their 5th title and a 9th Triple Crown.

Table

Position	Nation	Games				Points			Table points
		Played	Won	Drawn	Lost	For	Against	Difference	
1	Wales	4	4	0	0	42	14	+28	8
2	England	4	3	0	1	34	14	+20	6
3	Ireland	4	2	0	2	26	33	−7	4
4	France	4	1	0	3	29	37	−8	2
5	Scotland	4	0	0	4	22	55	−33	0

Results

Scotland	11–13	France
England	6–8	Wales
France	8–11	Ireland
Wales	11–0	Scotland
Ireland	12–8	Scotland
Ireland	3–14	Wales
Scotland	3–19	England
Wales	9–5	France
England	3–0	Ireland
France	3–6	England

Nation	Venue	City	Captain
England	Twickenham	London	Nim Hall
France	Stade Olympiqu Yves-du-Manoir	Colombes	Guy Basquet
Ireland	Lansdowne Road	Dublin	Des O'Brien
Scotland	Murrayfield	Edinburgh	Peter Kininmonth/Arthur Dorward
Wales	National Stadium/St. Helens	Cardiff/Swansea	John Gwilliam

The Masters 1952

The 1952 Masters Tournament was the 16th Masters Tournament, held April 3–6 at Augusta National Golf Club in Augusta, Georgia.
In strong winds and cool temperatures on the final two days, Sam Snead held on to the lead and won the second of his three Masters titles, four strokes ahead of runner-up Jack Burke, Jr. It was the sixth of Snead's seven major titles.

Defending champion Ben Hogan hosted the first Masters Club dinner (popularly known as the Champions dinner). He was the co-leader with Snead after three rounds at 214 (–2), but shot a 79 (+7) on Sunday and finished seven strokes back.

With a Sunday gallery estimated at 18,000 patrons at five dollars each, the purse was doubled by the tournament committee to $20,000, with a winner's share of $4,000.

Place	Player	Country	Score	To par	Money ($)
1	**Sam Snead**	United States	70-67-77-72=286	−2	4,000
2	Jack Burke, Jr.	United States	76-67-78-69=290	+2	2,500
T3	Al Besselink	United States	70-76-71-74=291	+3	1,387
	Tommy Bolt	United States	71-71-75-74=291		
	Jim Ferrier	Australia	72-70-77-72=291		
6	Lloyd Mangrum	United States	71-74-75-72=292	+4	800
T7	Julius Boros	United States	73-73-76-71=293	+5	625
	Fred Hawkins	United States	71-73-78-71=293		
	Ben Hogan	United States	70-70-74-79=293		
	Lew Worsham	United States	71-75-73-74=293		

Augusta National Golf Club, sometimes referred to as Augusta or the National, is one of the most famous and exclusive golf clubs in the world, located in Augusta, Georgia, United States. Unlike most private clubs which operate as non-profits, Augusta National is a for-profit corporation, and it does not disclose its income, holdings, membership list, or ticket sales.

Founded by Bobby Jones and Clifford Roberts, the course was designed by Jones and Alister Mackenzie and opened for play in 1932. Since 1934, the club has played host to the annual Masters Tournament, one of the four major championships in professional golf, and the only major played each year at the same course. It was the top-ranked course in Golf Digest's 2009 list of America's 100 greatest courses and was the number ten-ranked course based on course architecture on Golf week Magazine's 2011 list of best classic courses in the United States.

Cheltenham Gold Cup 1952

Mont Tremblant was a French-bred, British-trained Thoroughbred racehorse who won the 1952 Cheltenham Gold Cup. Originally trained in France, he was switched to a British stable and made an immediate impact, defeating a strong field to win the Gold Cup as a six-year-old. In the following season he finished third in the King George VI Chase and fourth in the Gold Cup before producing arguably his best performance by running second under top weight in the Grand National. His later career was repeatedly interrupted by injury. In the 1951/52 National Hunt season Mont Tremblant was matched against more experienced competition. In February he won a valuable handicap chase at Kempton Park Racecourse, conceding weight to his rivals. Mon Tremblant remained in training for several years and finished fourth in the 1953 Gold Cup but suffered recurrent injury problems and never won again at the highest level.

Triple Crown

2,000 Guineas 1952

Thunderhead was a French Thoroughbred racehorse and sire, best known for winning the classic 2000 Guineas in 1952. He won once as a two-year-old and showed improved form in the spring of 1952, winning the Prix de Fontainebleau before recording an emphatic win over twenty-five opponents in the 2000 Guineas. He then finished second when favourite for the Poule d'Essai des Poulains and ran poorly when strongly-fancied for The Derby. He was later exported to South Africa where he had some success as a breeding stallion.

The Derby & St Leger 1952

Tulyar was an Irish bred, British-trained Thoroughbred racehorse and sire. He won The Derby, the St. Leger Stakes, the King George VI and Queen Elizabeth Stakes, the Ormonde Stakes and the Eclipse Stakes setting a record for a single season's earnings in England. He stood at stud in Ireland and America, but failed to live up to expectations as a sire.

At Epsom, Tulyar started at odds of 11/2 for the Derby after a "last-minute plunge" made him favourite. Ridden by Charlie Smirke, he took the lead two furlongs from the finish and held off the late challenge of Gay Time to win by half a length in a time of 2 minutes 36.4 seconds. Shortly before the race, Smirke had sent a telegram to the Press Club which read "On Wednesday I will be saying to you What did I Tulyar". Tulyar was led into the winner's enclosure by his owner's son Prince Aly Khan. In July, Tulyar moved down in distance for the Eclipse Stakes over ten furlongs at Sandown and won "easily" from his stable companion Mehmandar. Later in the same month he contested the second running of the King George VI and Queen Elizabeth Stakes at Ascot. He won a "thrilling race" by a neck from Gay Time with the future Washington, D.C. International winner Worden in third.

In September, Tulyar started 10/11 favourite for the St Leger at Doncaster. He won by three lengths from Kingsford and eleven others.

1952 British Grand Prix

The 1952 British Grand Prix was a Formula Two race held on the 19th July 1952 at Silverstone Circuit. It was race 5 of 8 in the 1952 World Championship of Drivers, in which each Grand Prix was run to Formula Two rules rather than the Formula One regulations normally used. New pit facilities had been built on the straight between Woodcote and Copse corners; the original pits were located between Abbey and Woodcote.

Final Placings

Pos	No	Driver	Constructor	Laps	Time/Retired	Grid	Points
1	15	Alberto Ascari	Ferrari	85	2:46:11	2	9
2	17	Piero Taruffi	Ferrari	84	+1 lap	3	6
3	9	Mike Hawthorn	Cooper-Bristol	83	+2 laps	7	4
4	6	Dennis Poore	Connaught-Lea Francis	83	+2 laps	8	3
5	5	Eric Thompson	Connaught-Lea Francis	82	+3 laps	9	2
6	16	Nino Farina	Ferrari	82	+3 laps	1	
7	8	Reg Parnell	Cooper-Bristol	82	+3 laps	6	
8	14	Roy Salvadori	Ferrari	82	+3 laps	19	
9	4	Ken Downing	Connaught-Lea Francis	82	+3 laps	5	
10	21	Peter Whitehead	Ferrari	81	+4 laps	20	

1952 Wimbledon Championships

The 1952 Wimbledon Championships took place on the outdoor grass courts at the All England Lawn Tennis and Croquet Club in Wimbledon, London, United Kingdom. The tournament was held from Monday 23rd June until Saturday 5th July 1952. It was the 66th staging of the Wimbledon Championships, and the third Grand Slam tennis event of 1952. Frank Sedgman and Maureen Connolly won the singles titles.

Men's Singles

In the 1952 Wimbledon Championships – Gentlemen's Singles tennis competition, number one seed Frank Sedgman defeated number two seed Jaroslav Drobný in the final, 4–6, 6–2, 6–3, 6–2 to win the title. Dick Savitt was the defending champion, but lost in the quarterfinals to Mervyn Rose. Drobný was representing Egypt, having defected from Czechoslovakia in 1949 and been offered Egyptian citizenship in 1950. It was his second Wimbledon men's singles final, and he defeating the number 5 and 6 seeds to get there.

Women's Singles

Maureen Connolly defeated Louise Brough in the final, 7–5, 6–3 to win the Ladies' Singles tennis title at the 1952 Wimbledon Championships. Doris Hart was the defending champion, but lost in the quarterfinals to Pat Todd.

Men's Doubles

Ken McGregor and Frank Sedgman successfully defended their title, defeating Vic Seixas and Eric Sturgess in the final, 6–3, 7–5, 6–4 to win the Gentlemen' Doubles tennis title at the 1952 Wimbledon Championship.

Women's Doubles

Shirley Fry and Doris Hart successfully defended their title, defeating Louise Brough and Maureen Connolly in the final, 8–6, 6–3 to win the Ladies' Doubles tennis title at the 1952 Wimbledon Championships.

Mixed Doubles

Frank Sedgman and Doris Hart successfully defended their title, defeating Enrique Morea and Thelma Long in the final, 4–6, 6–3, 6–4 to win the Mixed Doubles tennis title at the 1952 Wimbledon Championships.

Frank Sedgman

Maureen Connolly

BOOKS PUBLISHED IN 1952

Love for Lydia is a semi-autobiographical novel written by British author H. E. Bates, first published in 1952. Lydia Aspen, a seemingly shy girl from a wealthy but isolated background, is encouraged by her aunts, her new carers, to discover the delights of growing up. They entrust her education to Mr Richardson, the young apprentice for Evensford's local newspaper, who is sent to their house to "get a story" about the recent death of Lydia's father. Richardson's access to the Aspens is unusual, as they are rarely seen by anyone from the town and hide behind their stone walls and perimeter of trees; introducing Lydia to the town's inhabitants gives Richardson a great sense of pride. Visiting the Aspen estate also allows Richardson the chance to escape from the great engulfing vacuum of Evensford, with its endless stretch of factory roofs and back alleys. As Lydia and Richardson spend more time together, he realises that his initial concept of Lydia was wrong, that she is far from being shy, and is often impetuous and demanding and enjoys captivating the young men who become her companions. Richardson soon discovers that his promise to love her, no matter what she does to him, is going to push him beyond the pain and feelings he thinks he is capable of experiencing.

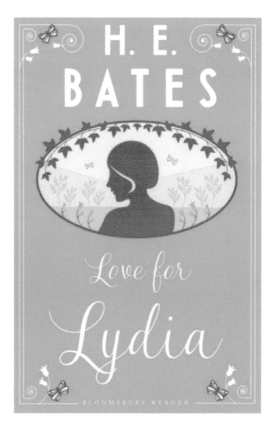

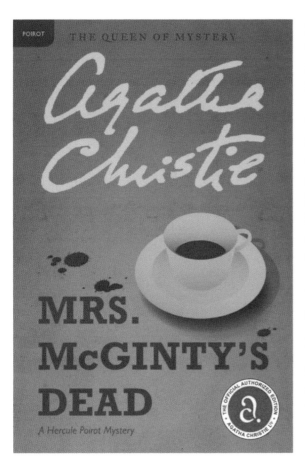

Mrs. McGinty's Dead is a work of detective fiction by British writer Agatha Christie, first published in the US by Dodd, Mead and Company in February 1952 and in the UK by the Collins Crime Club on the 3rd March the same year.

The novel features the characters Hercule Poirot and Ariadne Oliver. The story is a "village mystery", a subgenre of whodunit which Christie usually reserved for Miss Marple. The novel is notable for its wit and comic detail, something that had been little in evidence in the Poirot novels of the 1930s and 1940s. Poirot's misery in the run-down guesthouse, and Mrs Oliver's observations on the life of a detective novelist, provide considerable entertainment in the early part of the novel.

The publication of Mrs McGinty's Dead may be considered as marking the start of Poirot's final phase, in which Ariadne Oliver plays a large part. Although she had appeared in Cards on the Table in 1936, Mrs Oliver's most significant appearances in Christie's work begin here. She appears in five of the last nine Christie novels featuring Poirot, and appears on her own without Poirot at all in The Pale Horse.

They Do It with Mirrors is a detective fiction novel by British writer Agatha Christie, first published in the US by Dodd, Mead and Company in 1952 under the title of Murder with Mirrors and in UK by the Collins Crime Club on the 17th November that year under Christie's original title.

The US edition retailed at $2.50 and the UK edition at ten shillings and sixpence (10/6). The book features her detective Miss Marple.

One review at the time of publication praised the essence of the plot but felt the latter half of the novel moved too slowly. A later review considered that this novel showed "Definite signs of decline" and felt the author was not entirely comfortable with the setting she described in the novel.

In the text, Miss Marple says "they do it with mirrors": this is the slang term for the illusions of magicians and of a stage set. It is thinking of that which leads her to looking a new way at the evening of the first murder.

The novel's first proper adaptation was the 1985 television film Murder with Mirrors with Sir John Mills as Lewis Serrocold.

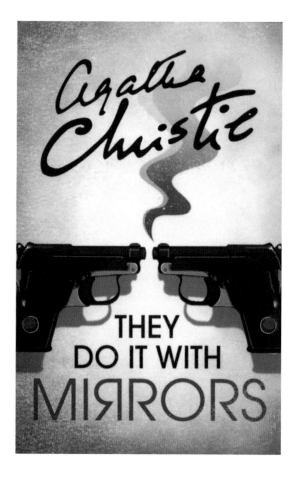

The Voyage of the Dawn Treader is a high fantasy novel for children by C. S. Lewis, published by Geoffrey Bles in 1952. It was the third published of seven novels in The Chronicles of Narnia (1950–1956) and Lewis had finished writing it in 1950, before the first book was out, It is volume five in recent editions, which are sequenced according to the novels' internal chronology. Like the others, it was illustrated by Pauline Baynes and her work has been retained in many later editions. It is the only Narnia book that does not have a main villain.

Lewis dedicated the book to Geoffrey Corbett. He is the foster-son of Owen Barfield, the friend, teacher, adviser and trustee of Lewis.

Macmillan US published an American edition within the calendar year with substantial revisions that were retained in the US until 1994.

The Voyage of the Dawn Treader has been adapted and filmed as four episodes of a BBC television series in 1989 and as a feature film in 2010.

The Borrowers is a children's fantasy novel by the English author Mary Norton, published by Dent in 1952. It features a family of tiny people who live secretly in the walls and floors of an English house and "borrow" from the big people in order to survive. The Borrowers also refers to the series of five novels including The Borrowers and four sequels that feature the same family after they leave "their" house.

The Borrowers won the 1952 Carnegie Medal from the Library Association, recognising the year's outstanding children's book by a British author. In the 70th anniversary celebration of the medal in 2007 it was named one of the top ten Medal-winning works, selected by a panel to compose the ballot for a public election of the all-time favourite.

Harcourt, Brace and Company published it in the U.S. in 1953 with illustrations by Beth and Joe Krush. It was also published in four parts, with illustrations by Erik Blegvad, during the summer of 1953 (June, July, August, September) in Woman's Day magazine. There have been several adaptations of The Borrowers in television and film.

EVELYN WAUGH

Sword of Honour

A FINAL VERSION OF
MEN AT ARMS
OFFICERS AND GENTLEMEN
UNCONDITIONAL SURRENDER

The Sword of Honour is a trilogy of novels by Evelyn Waugh which loosely parallel Waugh's experiences during Second World War. Published by Chapman & Hall from 1952 to 1961, the novels were: Men at Arms (1952); Officers and Gentlemen (1955); and Unconditional Surrender (1961), marketed as The End of the Battle in the United States and Canada.

The novels have obvious echoes in Evelyn Waugh's wartime career; his participation in the Dakar expedition, his stint with the commandos, his time in Crete and his role in Yugoslavia. Unlike Crouchback, Waugh was not a cradle Roman Catholic but a convert from the upper middle class – although Waugh clearly believed that the recusant experience was vital in the development of English Roman Catholicism.

The novel is the most thorough treatment of the theme of Waugh's writing, first fully displayed in Brideshead Revisited: a celebration of the virtues of tradition, of family and feudal loyalty, of paternalist hierarchy, of the continuity of institutions and of the heroic ideal and the calamitous disappearance of these which has led to the emptiness and futility of the modern world.

Ivanhoe. In the twelfth century, England is divided along ethno-religious lines, with the Saxons on one side and the Normans on the other. King Richard the Lionheart (Norman Wooland), who is supported by the Saxons, is kidnapped in returning from the Crusades. Against his father Cedric's (Finlay Currie's) orders leading to Cedric disowning him as a son, Sir Wilfred of Ivanhoe (Robert Taylor), one of Richard's knights and faithful subjects, goes in search of Richard, Ivanhoe's absence leading to speculation by the Normans that he is dead. Ivanhoe is able to locate Richard, who is being held captive by Leopold of Austria with the knowledge of Richard's brother, Prince John (Guy Rolfe), who has assumed the throne in Richard's absence with the support of the Normans. The ransom for Richard's release is the enormous sum of one hundred fifty marks of silver. Knowing that he cannot come up with that sum of silver through the Saxons alone, Ivanhoe approaches the Jews, led by Isaac (Felix Aylmer), for their support, despite the Jews being regarded as infidels.

Nominated for 3 Oscars

Run time is 1h 46mins

Trivia

At the beginning of this movie, Sir Wilfred of Ivanhoe is looking for King Richard I by singing until he finds the King. This is historically accurate, with the exception that the singer was a minstrel called Blondel. When Leopold of Austria captured King Richard I, Blondel went around to all of the castles singing King Richard's favourite song (one story had it that King Richard actually co-wrote the song). When he heard King Richard join in the chorus, he went home and told the Normans where King Richard was.

Released in the summer of 1952, this was MGM's highest grossing movie for the year and one of the top four money makers of 1952, grossing over $6.2 million. It took in $1,310,590 at the box office in 39 days of limited release, setting a record for an MGM movie. According to the "Motion Picture Almanac", it was the second highest-grossing movie of 1952, taking in more than $7 million.

Goofs

The opening credits feature a coat of arms of England supported on the dexter by a lion and an unicorn on the sinister. The unicorn from the arms of Scotland did not appear as a supporter of the arms of England until 1603, when the kingdoms of England and Scotland were united under King James I of England and VI of Scotland.

The shields in this film are made of metal and the heraldic charges are painted flat - a commonplace error in films. In Medieval Europe shields were made of wood and covered in dyed or painted leather. The charges were in relief, sculpted in gesso and coloured with paint.

During the fight scene in the dungeon, Cedric's costume clearly shows a zipper on the back.

The Bad And The Beautiful. Three successful movie industry people - an actress, a writer and a director - are invited to a major studio to hear a pitch from Jonathan Shields, an out of work movie producer to whom they all owe their success. In flashbacks, we learn how and why each of them has come to hate him completely. Fred Amiel, the director, was an assistant director until Shields gave him his big break; when he hires someone else to direct Amiel's dream project, it's the end. For Georgia Lorrison, an actress, Shields made her into a major star. When he pursues other women, it also marks the end of their professional relationship. For the writer, James Lee Bartlow, Shields plucked him out of some sleepy southern college town and turned one of his novels into a hit movie. Once again, Shields steps over the line when he arranges for a famous Latin movie star to squire Mrs. Bartlow around and tragedy ensues.

Box Office

Budget: $1,558,000 (estimated)
Cumulative Worldwide Gross: $2,025

Run time 1h 58mins

Trivia

To somewhat soften the depiction of Shields, Vincente Minnelli cut a scene in which he accepts the Best Picture Oscar® for the film whose idea he had stolen from his best friend. In the scene, Shields devotes most of his speech to his late father, and then makes only a brief mention of his friend at the end.

Sex is mentioned six times throughout the film. While this may not be a big deal today the filmmakers in 1952 had trouble getting the word to make it past the censors.

The character played by Kathleen Freeman was based on Alfred Hitchcock's wife, Alma Reville.

Kirk Douglas landed the lead role after Clark Gable had turned it down.

Goofs

In the Lorrison house, Jonathan cuts a drawing from the wallpaper and holds it unrolled, but it is half rolled-up in the next shot.

Jonathan coaches Georgia on how to seductively light a cigarette for her movie role but her part is in a historical picture in which she apparently plays a peasant/princess living in an era when women didn't smoke anyway, let alone use a cigarette as part of romantic allure.

When Jonathan is shining the flashlight at the girl in the attic (Georgia), at one point he aims it away from her, but the light remains steadily focused on her legs.

When we see Jonathan driving a car for the first time, he drives on the left-hand side of the road.

Singing In The Rain. 1927 Hollywood. Monumental Pictures' biggest stars, glamorous on-screen couple Lina Lamont and Don Lockwood, are also an off-screen couple if the trade papers and gossip columns are to be believed. Both perpetuate the public perception if only to please their adoring fans and bring people into the movie theatres. In reality, Don barely tolerates her, while Lina, despite thinking Don beneath her, simplemindedly believes what she sees on screen in order to bolster her own stardom and sense of self-importance. R.F. Simpson, Monumental's head, dismisses what he thinks is a flash in the pan: talking pictures. It isn't until The Jazz Singer (1927) becomes a bona fide hit which results in all the movie theatres installing sound equipment that R.F. knows Monumental, most specifically in the form of Don and Lina; have to jump on the talking picture bandwagon, despite no one at the studio knowing anything about the technology.

Box Office
Budget:$2,540,800 (estimated)
Gross USA: $1,826,108
Cumulative Worldwide Gross: $1,865,056

Run time 1h 23mins.

Trivia

For the "Make 'em Laugh" number, Gene Kelly asked Donald O'Connor to revive a trick he had done as a young dancer: running up a wall and completing a somersault. The number was so physically taxing that O'Connor, who smoked four packs of cigarettes a day at the time, ended up in a hospital bed for a week after its completion. He suffered from exhaustion and painful carpet burns. Unfortunately, an accident ruined all of the initial footage, so after a brief rest O'Connor--ever the professional--agreed to do the difficult number all over again.

Debbie Reynolds remarked many years later that making this movie and surviving childbirth were the two hardest things she'd ever had to do. The filming experience was particularly unpleasant due to her harsh treatment by perfectionist Gene Kelly. Decades later, Kelly expressed remorse about his behaviour: "I wasn't nice to Debbie. It's a wonder she still speaks to me."

Goofs

When Lina meets Don at the R.F. Simpson's party after the big premiere of "The Royal Rascal", she mentions something like "I didn't see you last night at Wally Reid's party". Wallace Reid died in 1923 and the action of the film is set in 1927.

If you listen carefully to the soundtrack as Gene Kelly tap dances in the rain, (actually Carol Haney tapping) you hear additional taps after Kelly stops dancing.

Cosmo's violin bow breaks and the hairs can be seen flapping about, yet when they finish the piece the bow is fixed.

When Don jumps off the trolley into Cathy's car, a wire supporting Don is visible.

Clash By Night. After ten long years of absence, Mae Doyle returns to her hometown of Monterey, California, disillusioned by the big-city lifestyle of New York. There, unattainable Mae's air of sophistication and confidence catches the eye of the hard-working, good-natured fisherman, Jerry, and his misogynistic, patronising, movie projectionist friend, Earl, who, right from the start, begins to court her. But, Mae has had her share of loser boyfriends, and even though she seems determined to spare an innocent her cynicism, she decides to take a second chance at love and marries Jerry. Now, one year and a baby daughter later, a silent undercurrent of unspoken desires and raw lust threaten Jerry's happiness. Once, Jerry promised that he would do anything for Mae. Is he prepared to lose everything in the aftermath of love?

Director: Fritz Lang
Writers: Alfred Hayes (screenplay), Clifford Odets (play)
Stars: Barbara Stanwyck, Robert Ryan, Paul Douglas.

Run time 1h 45mins

Trivia
As this was one of Marilyn Monroe's first starring roles, she was still under an acting coach and wanted her on the set to help her in scenes. She would stand behind director Fritz Lang and tell her when a scene was good enough, as opposed to listening to Lang, and when the director saw what was going on he got furious and demanded she leave the set (at the time this coach also worked for 20th Century Fox). After Monroe complained and wouldn't act without her, Lang allowed the coach to return to the set, on the condition that she not directs Monroe.

During the fight in the projection room, the theme song from another RKO film shot in 1951, The Las Vegas Story can be heard coming from the theatre.

Goofs
At the ~13 minute mark, after Mae walks past Joe in the Doyle house (Joe: "It's your life." Mae: "Yes, that's what's so funny. It's really mine."), you can see the moving shadow of one of the crew at the bottom left of the screen, on the floor.

At the beach Earl asks Mae...."Where did you get those blue, blue eyes?" Barbara Stanwyck in fact had brown eyes.

During the tavern scene, Mae and Jerry watch the moon rise over the ocean. The film takes place in Monterey, California, which is on the West coast, where the moon rises over the hills, and sets on the ocean.

When Earl is trying to hand Jerry money to pay his father's bar tab, the condition of the bills and the way they are held in Earl's hand change between perspective shots.

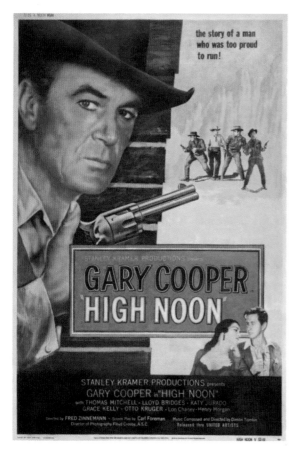

High Noon. Still in his impeccable wedding suit, the blissful newlywed and Hadleyville's retiring lawman, Marshal Will Kane, receives news that his implacable nemesis, Frank Miller, a convicted murderer, has been pardoned. Due in on the noon train, Miller is hell-bent on keeping his word: kill the man who put him behind bars, with the help of his murderous, three-member gang. But, bound by his noble, high moral principles, Kane refuses to hand in his tin star, against the will of his pacifist Quaker wife, Amy Fowler, only to face the inhabitants' shocking unwillingness to stand by him. Now, one man must face Miller and his killers alone. Who shall live, and who shall die in the duel at high noon?

Winner of four Oscars	Best Actor in a Leading Role
	Best Film Editing
	Best Music, Original Song
	Best Music, Scoring of a Dramatic or Comedy Picture

Box Office
Budget: $730,000 (estimated)

Run time 1h 25mins

Trivia

In 1951, after 25 years in show business, Gary Cooper's professional reputation was in decline, and he was dropped from the Motion Picture Herald's list of the top ten box-office performers. In the following year he made a big comeback, at the age of 51, with this film.

Lee Van Cleef was originally hired to play Deputy Marshal Harvey Pell. However, producer Stanley Kramer decided that his nose was too "hooked", which made him look like a villain, and told him to get it fixed. Van Cleef refused, and Lloyd Bridges got the part. Van Cleef was given the smaller role of gunman Jack Colby, one of the Miller gang.

Gary Cooper and Grace Kelly had an affair that lasted for the duration of filming.

Goofs

In the climactic crane shot when Kane is alone in the town square, modern-day buildings, high-voltage power lines, and telephone poles are clearly visible in the skyline.

In the two shots where we see Kane and then Harvey enter the livery, the sky is covered with clouds. In all other scenes, the sky is clear.

When the three friends of Miller are arriving by horse at the train station, an airplane is visible in the sky as the last rider crosses the tracks.

Due to weather problems, the climactic crane shot at "high noon" was actually taken at 3:00 pm, so the shadows are wrong for a "high-noon" shot.

The Quiet Man. Following a professional incident, Sean Thornton voluntarily decides to cut his chosen career short, and leave his Pittsburgh base to return to his Irish homeland, specifically Inisfree where he was born, has not been since he was a child and knows no one. Without knowing the situation before his arrival, he plans to buy and live in the cottage where he and seven generations of Thorntons before him were born to farm the land. Immediately upon his arrival, he falls in love at first sight with feisty local spinster, Mary Kate Danaher, who in turn is quietly and cautiously attracted to this stranger. If a courtship is to happen between the two of them, they must go through the official and traditional channels of rural Ireland. Thus, their possible courtship could be threatened by Mary Kate's eldest brother, Will Danaher, not giving his consent, as an issue has placed Sean in Will's bad books. The rest of the community, who like Sean and want to see a Sean and Mary Kate union, try to help them get Will's consent, but in the process they may further threaten the romance based on Mary Kate's traditional versus Sean's modern approach to marriage, in combination with the reason Sean left his American life behind, about which he has told no one in Inisfree.

Run time 2h 09mins

Trivia

In the scene where John Wayne discovers Maureen O'Hara in his cottage, the wind whipped her hair so ferociously around her face she kept squinting. John Ford screamed at her in the strongest language to open her eyes. "What would a bald-headed son of a bitch know about hair lashing across his eyeballs," she shot back.

In an interview John Wayne said that the final fight scene was stylized to make it seem more interesting. The fighters use long, swinging "roundhouse" punches rather than the economical short punches a real prize-fighter would use.

It is alleged that when Maureen O'Hara passed away in 2015, she did so listening to Victor Young's score to the film.

Goofs

When the men at the bar sing "Wild Colonial Boy" for the second time, it actually looks like they are singing a different song. Their lips are totally out of sync with the audio/music.

John Wayne's wedding ring is clearly visible before he even meets Mary Kate Danniher. It is most clearly seen while he is remembering his mother's words before introducing himself to Michaleen.

After the wedding, when Sean & Mary Kate are back at the cottage & she storms out, it's dark outside but the birds are chirping away outside.

At the horse race there is a sign that says "Inishfree race meet". In Ireland they are called race meetings not meets.

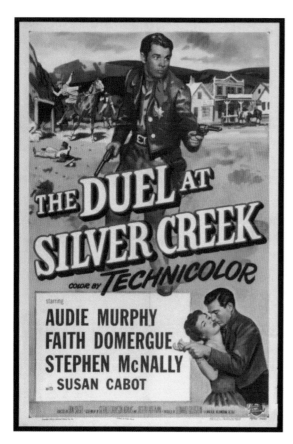

The Duel At Silver Creek. A gang of crooks are murdering miners for their gold claims. Luke Cromwell (Murphy) loses his father to the gang and quickly reinvents himself as a gambling gunslinger known as The Silver Kid. Down in Silver City, Marshal Lightning Tyrone (McNally) is determined to bring to justice the claim jumping murderers. But he has a problem, his trigger finger is inoperative after he was shot, thus he can't let the bad guys know he is no longer "Lightning" on the trigger. After witnessing some of The Silver Kid's handy work, Tyrone hires him as a deputy to watch his back as he sets about weeding out the bad in Silver City. Luke is only too happy to help; he wants vengeance for his father's murder. But two ladies in town are to have a big impact on both of their lives; the question is if both men can finally achieve their goals without further loss of life.

Brisk, colourful and highly entertaining Western fare for the undemanding matinée crowd. Forget all hopes of depth and intricate characterisations and expect an action packed shoot em' up instead.

Run time 1h 17mins

Trivia

The title is a bit of a misnomer, as a duel means two people, not a full-fledged gun battle involving well over a dozen men.

This was Don Siegel's first western, as well as his first film for Universal, which became his home studio in the '60s and '70s.

Goofs

During the climactic gunfight where rider Rod Lacy is himself chased on horseback by the marshal and both then dismount to continue shooting at each other, Lacy astonishingly manages to fire 11 shots from what is clearly a revolver pistol (which normally fires only 6) before an attempted 12th shot reveals it to be out of ammunition, and only then is Lacy forced to reload it - he is out of frame briefly whilst on his galloping horse (the camera cuts to the chasing marshal) but could not have conceivably re-loaded during that very short time, and at no point throughout is he shown to be carrying 2 guns.

At the film's climax, Gerald Mohr's six-shooter fires at least ten times before he finally reloads.

When we first meet Marshal Lightning Tyrone and his father, the tracks of the camera dolly are clearly visible as they walk through the town's main street.

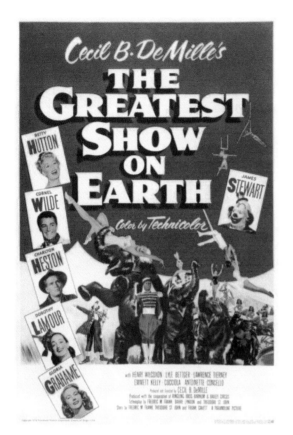

The Greatest Show on Earth is a 1952 American drama film produced and directed by Cecil B. DeMille, shot in Technicolor, and released by Paramount Pictures. Set in the Ringling Bros. and Barnum & Bailey Circus, the film stars Betty Hutton and Cornel Wilde as trapeze artists competing for the centre ring, and Charlton Heston as the circus manager running the show. James Stewart also stars in a supporting role as a mysterious clown who never removes his make-up, even between shows, while Dorothy Lamour and Gloria Grahame also play supporting roles.

In addition to the film actors, the real Ringling Bros. and Barnum & Bailey's Circus' 1951 troupe appears in the film, with its complement of 1,400 people, hundreds of animals, and 60 railroad cars of equipment and tents. The actors learned their respective circus roles and participated in the acts. The film's storyline is supported by lavish production values; actual circus acts; and documentary, behind-the-rings looks at the complex logistics that made big top circuses possible.

Run time 2h 32mins

Trivia

Cecil B. DeMille was always demanding of his actors and actresses. He insisted that everyone truly learn to perform the circus stunts they were supposed to be performing. This meant that Betty Hutton really learned the trapeze and Gloria Grahame had to let an elephant rest its foot an inch from her face. Cornel Wilde probably had it the worst, since he was portraying a high-wire artist. He was seriously afraid of heights.

Ex-trapeze artist Burt Lancaster was considered for Cornel Wilde's role, as was Kirk Douglas. Both subsequently played trapeze artists, Lancaster in Trapeze (1956) and Douglas in The Story of Three Loves (1953).

When Mary Pickford presented the film's producer-director Cecil B. DeMille with the Oscar for Best Picture, not only was it the first time the Academy Awards ceremonies had ever been televised, it was also Pickford's very first television appearance.

Goofs

When Mickey Mouse and other Walt Disney characters walk around the ring, the band plays the song "It's A Hap-Hap-Happy Day" from Gulliver's Travels, which was released by Paramount, not Disney.

When Brad is checking the baby gorillas after learning they may have contracted the mumps, a crowd of onlookers is gathered right behind, plainly staring at the camera filming the scene.

It's medically impossible to perform a blood transfusion by directly siphoning blood from one person to another through a tube, a procedure done here in that manner from Sebastian to Brad following the train wreck.

The success of the train robbery depends on the driver seeing a little flare (which burns for an incredibly long time). The robbers also believe the driver of the second section won't see a stopped train with elevated, large, red, lights. They are correct on both counts.

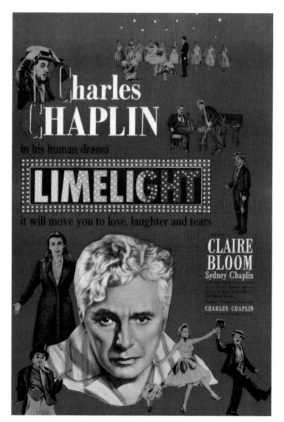

Limelight. The movie is set in London in 1914, on the eve of World War I, and the year Chaplin made his first film. Calvero (Charlie Chaplin), once a famous stage clown, but now a washed-up drunk, saves a young dancer, Thereza "Terry" Ambrose (Claire Bloom), from a suicide attempt. Nursing her back to health, Calvero helps Terry regain her self-esteem and resume her dancing career. In doing so, he regains his own self-confidence, but an attempt to make a comeback is met with failure. Terry says she wants to marry Calvero despite their age difference; however, she has befriended Neville (Sydney Earl Chaplin), a young composer who Calvero believes would be better suited to her. In order to give them a chance, Calvero leaves home and becomes a street entertainer. Terry, now starring in her own show, eventually finds Calvero and persuades him to return to the stage for a benefit concert. Reunited with an old partner (Buster Keaton), Calvero gives a triumphant comeback performance. He suffers a heart attack during a routine, however, and dies in the wings while watching Terry, the second act on the bill, dance on stage.

Run time 2h 17mins

Trivia

The flea circus act in the film was a comedy idea that Charles Chaplin had conceived of in 1919. Originally, he used it in the one completed scene of an aborted film project called The Professor (1919). Later, he attempted to use the idea for The Circus (1928) and The Great Dictator (1940), but could not justify it in either plot. Finally, in this film he was able to use the act.

Charles Chaplin, Ray Rasch, and Larry Russell won the Oscar for Best Original Score for this film, but it was the Oscar for films released in 1972. The picture had never played in a Los Angeles-area cinema during the intervening 20 years and was not eligible for Oscar consideration until it did.

The Academy Award that Charles Chaplin won for composing this film's score is the only competitive Oscar he ever received; his other awards were given to him for special achievement outside of the established categories.

Goofs

The letter Calvero receives from Redfern states that his performance at Middlesex is on Monday 5th September. In 1914, when the scene is supposed to take place, 5th September was a Saturday.

The film begins in the summer of 1914, as the First World War began, but less than a year passes before a newsboy shows a headline "United States Enters War", which didn't happen until April 1917, and Neville is drafted, though the draft did not begin until 1916. Curiously, only one person appears in uniform, despite England being on a war footing.

In the dressing room scene with his partner, Calvero is darkening his left eyebrow. When a visitor enters the room, a quick shot of Calvero reveals both eyebrows darkened. As the conversation continues with his partner, Calvero's right eyebrow remains untouched.

Moulin Rouge. In 1890 Paris crowds pour into the Moulin Rouge nightclub as artist Henri de Toulouse-Lautrec finishes a bottle of cognac while sketching the club's dancers. The club's regulars arrive: singer Jane Avril teases Henri charmingly, dancers La Goulue and Aicha fight, and owner Maurice Joyant offers Henri free drinks for a month in exchange for painting a promotional poster. At closing time, Henri waits for the crowds to disperse before standing to reveal his four-foot six-inch stature. As he walks to his Montmartre apartment, he recalls the events that led to his disfigurement. In flashbacks it is revealed that Henri was a bright, happy child, cherished by his parents, the fabulously wealthy Count and Countess de Toulouse-Lautrec. But as a boy Lautrec fell down a flight of stairs and his legs failed to heal because of a genetic weakness, likely resulting from his parents being first cousins. His legs stunted and pained, Henri loses himself in his art, while his father leaves his mother to ensure that they have no more children. As a young adult, Henri proposes to the woman he loves but, when she tells him that no woman will ever love him, he leaves his childhood home in despair to begin a new life as a painter in Paris.

Run time 1h 59mins

Trivia

Director John Huston only finished the final edit a few hours before the December premiere to qualify it for Academy Award consideration.

When director John Huston appeared on the BBC's "Desert Island Discs" program in 1973, host Roy Plomley told him that this movie was a personal favourite of his. Huston replied "I don't think it's one of my best films", adding that 1950s censorship constraints had made it impossible to tell the story of Henri de Toulouse Lautrec's life honestly.

John Huston was disgusted by the French individualism during the shooting in Paris streets. Such as the bystanders who walked in the streets whilst the crew and actors trying to do their job.

For much of the film the 40-year-old José Ferrer was playing Henri de Toulouse Lautrec at the age of 25.

Peter Cushing and Christopher Lee appeared together once before. The next twenty times they were the most successful stars in horror films.

Colette Marchand was the only Best Actress in a Supporting Role Oscar nominee that year that was from a Best Picture nominated movie.

Goofs

When Henri Lautrec arrives at the gallery for the showing of his pictures, as he 'walks' in, his shadow on the ground clearly shows Jose Ferrer's legs tucked behind him as he walks (on his knees).

When Henri falls down the stairs toward the end of the film, his legs suddenly appear regular sized.

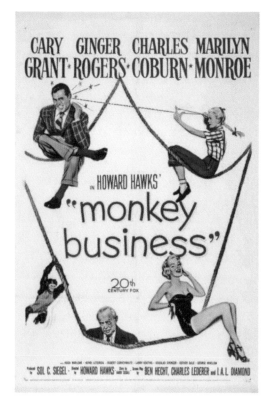

Monkey Business. Dr. Barnaby Fulton (Cary Grant), an absent-minded research chemist for the Oxly chemical company, is trying to develop an elixir of youth. He is urged on by his commercially minded boss, Oliver Oxly (Charles Coburn). One of Dr. Fulton's chimpanzees, Esther, gets loose in the laboratory, mixes a beaker of chemicals, and pours the mix into the water cooler. The chemicals have the rejuvenating effect Fulton is seeking. Unaware of Esther's antics, Fulton tests his latest experimental concoction on himself and washes it down with water from the cooler. He soon begins to act like a 20-year-old and spends the day out on the town with his boss's secretary, Lois Laurel (Marilyn Monroe). When Fulton's wife, Edwina (Ginger Rogers), learns that the elixir "works", she drinks some along with water from the cooler and turns into a prank-pulling schoolgirl.

Edwina makes an impetuous phone call to her old flame, the family lawyer, Hank Entwhistle (Hugh Marlowe). Her mother, who knows nothing of the elixir, believes that Edwina is truly unhappy in her marriage and wants a divorce.

Run time 1h 37mins

Trivia

The car used in the film was a red 1952 MG TD Roadster, which was owned by Marilyn Monroe. It sustained a dent in the front bumper when Cary Grant drove the car and hit a fence. Later purchased by Debbie Reynolds in a pre-sale at a 20th Century Fox studio auction, and then stored for several years. In 2011 it was sold at auction for $210,000.

Among the movie star photos Marilyn Monroe taped to her bedroom wall when she was a foster child were several of Cary Grant, with whom she was thrilled to be co-starring in this film, a break-through role in her then fast-rising movie career.

The neighbourhood through which Cary Grant and Marilyn Monroe go joy-riding in an MG sports car before crashing into a moving van is Brentwood, California, which is immediately adjacent to the 20th Century-Fox back-lot where this film was shot.

Goofs

When Barnaby and Lois leave the car lot in his new car, they cut in front of a large truck that turns off the street as they enter it. Further down the road they are seen passing the very same truck off the left side of the road.

When the kids tie up Hugh Marlowe, his coat is bungled up in the rope. After the cut when Grant comes out of the woods, the coat is smoothed out and the ropes are completely different around Marlowe.

Scientists refer to chimpanzees as monkeys. Chimpanzees are apes, not monkeys.

On one occasion, in the last reel, Oxley addresses Lois as 'Miss Monroe' rather than 'Miss Laurel'

After Hugh Marlowe has been "scalped", he is wearing a 'mohawk skull cap' which wrinkles up when he turns his head.

MUSIC 1952

Artist	Single	Reached number one	Weeks at number one
1952			
Teresa Brewer	Longing for You	10th November 1951	9
Mario Lanza	The Loveliest Night of the Year	12th January 1952	1
Teresa Brewer	Longing for You	19th January 1952	2
Mario Lanza	The Loveliest Night of the Year	2rd February 1952	3
Guy Mitchell	There's Always Room at Our House	23th February 1952	4
Nat "King" Cole	Unforgettable	22nd March 1952	9
Jo Stafford	A-Round the Corner	24th May 1952	3
Vera Lynn	Auf Wiederseh'n Sweetheart	14th June 1952	10
Vera Lynn	The Homing Waltz	23rd August 1952	9
Al Martino	Here in My Heart	25th October 1952	12

The UK Singles Chart is the official record chart in the United Kingdom. Record charts in the UK began life in 1952 when Percy Dickins from New Musical Express (NME) imitated an idea started in American Billboard magazine and began compiling a hit parade. Prior to this, a song's popularity was measured by the sales of sheet music. Initially, Dickins telephoned a sample of around 20 shops asking for a list of the 10 best-selling songs. These results were then aggregated to give a Top 12 chart published in NME on the 14th November 1952. The number-one single was "Here in My Heart" by Al Martino.

According to The Official Charts Company and Guinness' British Hit Singles & Albums, the NME is considered the official British singles chart before 10th March 1960. However, until 15th February 1969, when the British Market Research Bureau chart was established, there was no universally accepted chart. Other charts existed and different artists may have placed at number one in charts by Record Mirror, Disc or Melody Maker. Alternatively, some considered BBC's Pick of the Pops, which averaged all these charts, to be a better indicator of the number-one single.

Teresa Brewer

" Longing for you "

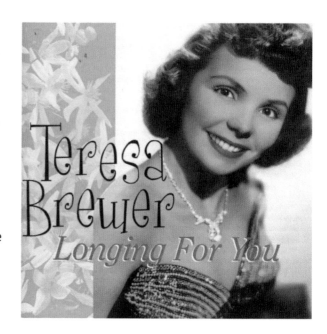

"Longing for You" Teresa Brewer born Theresa Veronica Breuer was an American singer whose style incorporated pop, country, jazz, R&B, musicals, and novelty songs. She was one of the most prolific and popular female singers of the 1950s, recording nearly 600 songs. In 1949 she recorded the song Copenhagen (a jazz perennial) with the Dixieland All-Stars. For the B side she recorded the song "Music! Music! Music!" Unexpectedly, it was not the A side but the B side which took off, selling over a million copies and becoming Teresa's signature song. Another novelty song, "Choo'n Gum", hit the top 20 in 1950, followed by "Molasses, Molasses". Although she preferred to sing ballads, her only recorded ballad to make the charts was "Longing for You" in 1951. It reached number one on the 10th November 1951 and stayed there for 9 weeks.

Mario Lanza

"The Loveliest Night of the Year"

"The Loveliest Night of the Year" Mario Lanza recorded the song. It became one of the most popular songs of 1951, reaching number three in the US Billboard Charts. Lanza received his third Gold Disc for this song. In the UK, the song was a number one hit based on sales of sheet music. It reached the top spot in January 1952, staying there for four weeks. The song was also associated with Anne Shelton, whose contemporary recording was available alongside Lanza's.

The instrumental version of the song is often associated with magicians performing their "magical tricks", and flying trapeze acts, with whom it is often played in the background, especially in animated cartoons. It is as commonly associated with these entertainments as to be iconic, although few people know it the music by name.

Guy Mitchell

"There's Always Room at Our House"

"There's Always Room at Our House "Guy Mitchell was born Albert George Cernik and was an American pop singer and actor, successful in his homeland, the UK, and Australia. He sold 44 million records, including six million-selling singles.

Mitch Miller, in charge of talent at Columbia Records, noticed Cernik in 1950. He joined Columbia and took his new stage name at Miller's urging: Miller supposedly said, "my name is 'Mitchell' and you seem a nice 'guy', so we'll call you Guy Mitchell." Bob Merrill wrote hits for Mitchell.

Born of Croatian immigrants in Detroit, Michigan, at age 11 he was signed by Warner Brothers Pictures, to be a child star, and performed on the radio on KFWB in Los Angeles, California.

Nat King Cole

"Unforgettable"

The Unforgettable
Nat King Cole

"Unforgettable" is a popular song written by Irving Gordon and produced by Lee Gillette. The song's original working title was "Uncomparable"; however, the music publishing company asked Gordon to change it to "Unforgettable". The song was published in 1951. The most popular version of the song was recorded by Nat King Cole in 1951 from his album Unforgettable (1952), with an arrangement written by Nelson Riddle. A non-orchestrated version of the song recorded in 1952 is featured as one of the seven bonus tracks on Cole's 1998 CD reissue of 1955's otherwise completely instrumental album, Penthouse Serenade. The song also won three awards at the 34th Annual Grammy Awards (1992): Song of the Year, Record of the Year and Best Traditional Pop Vocal Performance. Nat Cole's original recording was inducted into the Grammy Hall of Fame in 2000.

Jo Stafford

"Ay-round The Corner"

"A-round the Corner (Beneath the Berry Tree)", also titled "Ay-round the Corner (Bee-hind The Bush)" is a traditional popular song adapted by Josef Marais, from the repertoire of Marais and Miranda. The most popular version was recorded by Jo Stafford on 10 December 1951 with accompaniment by her partner Paul Weston and the Norman Luboff Choir.

It was issued on Columbia 39653 and entered the Billboard chart in March 1952, peaking at number nine, also making number 12 on the Cash Box chart. A recording by The Weavers and Gordon Jenkins on Decca charted in April and reached number 19. In the UK, the song entered the chart based on sheet music sales in April, and reached number one in May, holding the top spot for three weeks.

Vera Lynn

"Auf Wiederseh'n, Sweetheart"

"Auf Wiederseh'n, Sweetheart". The recording of the song by Vera Lynn, which featured accompaniment by Soldiers and Airmen of HM Forces and the Johnny Johnston Singers, was the first song recorded by a foreign artist to make number one on the U.S. Billboard charts, in 1952. Reaching the summit on the Billboard "Best Sellers in Stores" chart on the 12th July, the song spent nine weeks at No. 1. In reaching number-one, it would be almost six years before another British artist would top the U.S. pop chart; that song was Laurie London's "He's Got the Whole World in His Hands," in April 1958. Currently, "Auf Wiederseh'n Sweetheart" is tied with "Hey Jude" for third amongst longest-running number-one songs by British artists on the Billboard pop charts, behind "Candle in the Wind 1997"/"Something About the Way You Look Tonight" by Elton John (14 weeks, 1997-1998).

Vera Lynn

"The Homing Waltz"

"The Homing Waltz" is a song that was written by Johnny Reine and Tommie Connor and recorded by Vera Lynn in 1952. It charted at a peak position of number nine on the UK Singles Chart. The tune was that of the cowboy folksong "The Streets of Laredo".

The song reached number one in the UK's sheet music charts in August 1952, where it stayed for nine weeks. It was replaced by Al Martino's "Here in My Heart", which became the inaugural number one on the first UK Singles Chart based on record sales, published on the 14th November 1952.

On this chart, "The Homing Waltz" was at number nine. Another contemporary recording available was by the up-and-coming young British singer Alma Cogan.

Al Martino

"Here In My Heart"

"Here in My Heart" is a popular song, written by Pat Genaro, Lou Levinson, and Bill Borrelli, and published in 1952.

A recording of the song by Al Martino made history as the first number one on the UK Singles Chart, on the 14th November 1952. "Here in My Heart" remained in the top position for nine weeks in the United Kingdom, setting a record for the longest consecutive run at number one, a record which, over 50 years on, has only been beaten by eight other tracks - Bryan Adams's "(Everything I Do) I Do It for You" (16 weeks), the Wet Wet Wet version of The Troggs' "Love Is All Around" (15 weeks).

Mario Lanza, at the height of his popularity in the early 1950, had also planned to record this song, but changed his mind when asked not to by Martino, so his recording would not be overlooked.

WORLD EVENTS 1952

January

1st Mail subsidies to National Airlines end, and the United States Post Office Department places the airline on a mail service rate that makes it self-sustaining throughout its system.

6th Charles M. Schulz' Peanuts receives its first Sunday comics page.

8th West Germany has 8 million refugees inside its borders.

10th "The Greatest Show on Earth", directed and produced by Cecil B. DeMille, starring James Stewart and Charlton Heston, premieres in New York.

12th The University of Tennessee admits its first African-American student.

14th Rationing of coffee in Netherlands ends.

20th The NBA's first superstar George Mikan scores a career high 61 points leading the Minneapolis Lakers to a 91-81 double-overtime victory over the Rochester Royals.

23rd On the night of 23–24 January 1952 the Port Martin base was largely destroyed by a fire which burnt down its main building. No lives were lost nor injuries incurred but the base personnel were evacuated to Petrel Island, where they overwintered, and Port Martin abandoned.

26th The Cairo fire also known as Black Saturday, was a series of riots that took place on the 26th January 1952, marked by the burning and looting of some 750 buildings—retail shops, cafes, cinemas, hotels, restaurants, theatres, nightclubs, and the city's Opera House—in downtown Cairo. The direct trigger of the riots was the killing by British occupation troops of 50 Egyptian auxiliary policemen in the city of Ismaïlia in a massacre one day earlier. The spontaneous anti-British protests that followed these deaths were quickly seized upon by organized elements in the crowd, who burned and ransacked large sectors of Cairo amidst the unexplained absence of security forces. The fire is thought by some to have signalled the end of the Kingdom of Egypt. The perpetrators of the Cairo Fire remain unknown to this day, and the truth about this important event in modern Egyptian history has yet to be established.

January

28th Australian Championships Women's Tennis: In an all-Australian final Thelma Coyne Long beats Helen Angwin 6-2, 6-3 for 1st of her 2 Australian singles titles.

Australian Championships Men's Tennis: Ken McGregor wins his first and only Grand Slam event; upsets fellow Australian Frank Sedgman 7-5, 12-10, 2-6, 6-2.

February

2nd The extraordinary 1952 Groundhog Day Storm was the only Atlantic tropical cyclone on record in February. First observed in the western Caribbean Sea on February 2 as a non-frontal low, it moved rapidly throughout its duration and struck southwestern Florida early the next day as a gale-force storm. In the state, the winds damaged some crops and power lines, but no serious damage was reported. The system became a tropical storm after emerging over the Atlantic Ocean before quickly transitioning into an extratropical cyclone on February 4. Strong winds and waves washed a freighter ashore, but no injuries were related to the event. Subsequently, the storm brushed eastern New England, causing minor power outages, before it moved inland near Maine. There were no reported fatalities related to the storm.

13th Future world champion Rocky Marciano knocks out Italian heavyweight boxer Gino Buonvino in the 2nd round at Rhode Island Auditorium, Providence for his 40th straight win.

Rocky Marciano

Gino Buonvino

14th Giant slalom event for women debuts at the Winter Olympics at Oslo Games; American skier Andrea Mead-Lawrence wins gold ahead of Dagmar Rom of Austria and German Annemarie Buchner.

15th King George VI is buried in St. George's Chapel, Windsor Castle, England.

16th | United States goes 1-2 in the 500m speed skating at the Olso Winter Olympics with Ken Henry taking gold ahead of teammate Don McDermott; Norwegian Hjalmar Anderson dominates remaining 3 speed skating events.

18th | The 4th Emmy Awards, retroactively known as the 4th Primetime Emmy Awards after the debut of the Daytime Emmy Awards, were presented at the Cocoanut Grove in Los Angeles, California on the 18th February 1952. The ceremonies were hosted by Lucille Ball and Desi Arnaz. This was the first year that nominations were considered on a national television network basis. Previously, the Emmys were primarily given out to shows that were produced or aired in the Los Angeles area.

20th | "African Queen" film directed by John Huston, starring Humphrey Bogart and Katharine Hepburn is released in the US.

22nd | Germany takes the Olympic bobsleigh double with gold in the 4-man event at the Oslo Winter Games; Adreas Ostler and Lorenz Niebert score their 2nd gold medals after winning the 2-man a week earlier.

23rd | Lydia Wideman of Finland becomes first female Olympic cross-country skiing champion; wins inaugural 10k event in Olso; Finnish medal sweep with minors to Mirja Hietamies and Siiri Rantanen.

24th | Canada wins 6th Olympic ice hockey title courtesy of a final round 3-3 tie with the US at the Oslo Winter Games; Canadian centre Billy Gibson top scores with 19 points.

25th | VI Winter Olympic Games close at Oslo, Norway.

29th | Ice Dance Championship at Paris France won by Westwood & Demmy of Great Britain.

March

1st   Egyptian government-Ali Maher Pasha resigns.

3rd   Puerto Rico approves its 1st self-written constitution.

5th   The Deep Blue Sea is a British stage play by Terence Rattigan from the 5th March 1952. Rattigan based his story and characters in part on his secret relationship with Kenny Morgan, and the aftermath of the end of their relationship. The play was first performed in London on 6 March 1952, directed by Frith Banbury, and won praise for actress Peggy Ashcroft, who co-starred with Kenneth More. In the US, the Plymouth Theatre staged the play in October 1952, with Margaret Sullavan. The play with Sullavan subsequently transferred to Broadway, with its Broadway premiere on 5 November 1953, and running for 132 performances.

10th   General Fulgencio Batista re-takes power in Cuba in a coup.

15th   73 inches (1,870 mm) of rain falls in Cilaos, Réunion, the most rainfall in one day up to that time.

16th   LPGA Titleholders Championship Women's Golf, Augusta CC: Babe Didrikson Zaharias wins her 3rd Titleholders title by 7 strokes from Betsy Rawls.

Babe Didrikson Zaharias

Betsy Rawls

20th   24th Academy Awards: "An American in Paris", Humphrey Bogart & Vivian Leigh win.

     The United States Senate ratifies a peace treaty with Japan.

21st   The last persons to be executed under military law were SS officers Andries Jan Pieters and Artur Albrecht on the 21st March 1952. Capital punishment remained a legal military option until 1983 when it was explicitly forbidden in the Constitution of the Netherlands. In 1991, all references to the death penalty were removed from Dutch law.

22nd   Wernher von Braun publishes the first in his series of articles titled Man Will Conquer Space Soon! including ideas for crewed flights to Mars and the Moon.

March

23rd New York Rangers blow 6-2 lead, lose 7-6 to Chicago Black Hawks; Bill Mosienko scores fastest hat trick in NHL history, 21 seconds.

27th Israel's former prime minister Menachem Begin was involved in a plot to blow up West Germany's first post-war chancellor, Konrad Adenauer. The respected Frankfurter Allgemeine Zeitung claimed that the Zionist leader approved and helped organise the assassination attempt using a bomb hidden in an encyclopaedia, even offering to sell his gold watch as the conspirators ran out of money. The bomb, arranged in March 1952, was detected before it reached Adenauer, but exploded killing a disposal expert and injuring two of his colleagues. French detectives arrested five Israeli people in Paris, all of whom were members of the Zionist group Irgun Tsvai Leumi, which Begin was linked to.

"Singin' in the Rain", musical comedy directed by Gene Kelly and Stanley Donen, starring Gene Kelly and Debbie Reynolds, premieres at Radio City Music Hall in NYC.

28th US Ladies' Figure Skating championship won by Tenley Albright and US Men's Figure Skating championship was won by Richard Button.

30th 6th Tony Awards: "The Fourposter" and "The King & I" win.

April

1st US performs nuclear test at Nevada Test Site.

6th 16th US Masters Tournament, Augusta National GC: Sam Snead wins his second green jacket by 4 strokes over Jack Burke Jr.

7th The American Research Bureau reports that the I Love Lucy episode, "The Marriage License", was the first TV show in history to be seen in around 10,000,000 homes, the evening the episode aired.

8th The U.S. Supreme Court limits the power of the President to seize private business, after President Harry S. Truman nationalizes all steel mills in the United States, just before the 1952 steel strike begins.

9th Hugo Ballivián's government is overthrown by the Bolivian National Revolution, which starts a period of agrarian reform, universal suffrage and the nationalization of tin mines.

April

15th The United States B-52 Stratofortress flies for the first time. The Boeing B-52 Stratofortress is an American long-range, subsonic, jet-powered strategic bomber. The B-52 was designed and built by Boeing, which has continued to provide support and upgrades. It has been operated by the United States Air Force (USAF) since the 1950s. The bomber is capable of carrying up to 70,000 pounds (32,000 kg) of weapons and has a typical combat range of more than 8,800 miles (14,080 km) without aerial refuelling.

16th "4 Saints in 3 Acts" opens at Broadway Theatre NYC for 15 performances.

18th West Germany and Japan form diplomatic relations.

21st Secretaries' Day (now Administrative Professionals' Day) is first celebrated.

23rd The Kirkuk–Baniyas pipeline is a crude oil pipeline from the Kirkuk oil field in Iraq to the Syrian port of Baniyas. The pipeline is around 800 kilometres (500 mi) long and the capacity is 300 thousand barrels per day (48×103 m3/d). The pipeline was opened on the 23rd April 1952. During the 2003 invasion of Iraq, the pipeline was damaged by U.S. air-strikes and remained out of operation since then.

On 17th December 2007, Syria and Iraq agreed to rehabilitate the pipeline. The pipeline was to be reconstructed by Stroytransgaz, a subsidiary of Gazprom. However, Stroytransgaz failed to start the rehabilitation and the contract was nullified in April 2009. As the rehabilitation of the existing pipeline occurred to be more costly than building a new pipeline, in September 2010 Iraq and Syria agreed to build two new Kirkuk–Baniyas pipelines. One pipeline with capacity of 1.5 million barrels per day (240×103 m3/d) would carry heavier crude oil while another pipeline capacity of 1.25 million barrels per day (199×103 m3/d) would carry lighter crude oil.

25th American Bowling Congress approves use of an automatic pinsetter for tenpin bowling.

26th On this day, In 1952 Patty Berg shot a 64 during the Richmond Open which was, at the time, the lowest score ever posted by a woman in golf. She did it over the 6,339 yard Richmond layout from the regulation tees. She shot a 30 on the front nine and a 34on the back for a total of 64.

28th After winning the 1952 New Hampshire primary, Eisenhower resigned from his NATO command and returned to the United States. He went on to win the 1952 presidential election, and served as the 34th President of the United States from 1953 to 1961.

April

28th | The Treaty of San Francisco goes into effect, formally ending the war between Japan and the Allies, and simultaneously ending the occupation of the four main Japanese islands by the Supreme Commander for the Allied Powers.

29th | Lever House officially opens at 390 Park Avenue in New York City, heralding a new age of commercial architecture in the United States. Designed by Gordon Bunshaft of Skidmore, Owings & Merrill, it is the first International Style skyscraper.

30th | On the 30th April 1952, Mr. Potato Head became the first toy advertised on television. The campaign was also the first to be aimed directly at children; before this, commercials were only targeted at adults, so toy advertisements had always been pitched to parents.

May

1st | US Marines take part in an atomic explosion training in Nevada.

2nd | After its July 1949 test flight, the Comet underwent three more years of testing and training flights. Then, on the 2nd May 1952, the British Overseas Aircraft Corporation (BOAC) began the world's first commercial jet service with the 44-seat Comet 1A, flying paying passengers from London to Johannesburg.

3rd | U.S. lieutenant colonels Joseph O. Fletcher and William P. Benedict land a plane at the geographic North Pole.

5th | Pulitzer prize awarded to Herman Wouk for this novel "The Caine Mutiny". The novel grew out of Wouk's personal experiences aboard two destroyer-minesweepers in the Pacific Theatre in World War II. Among its themes, it deals with the moral and ethical decisions made at sea by ship captains. The mutiny of the title is legalistic, not violent, and takes place during Typhoon Cobra, in December 1944. The court-martial that results provides the dramatic climax to the plot.

7th | The concept of the integrated circuit, the basis for all modern computers, is first published by Geoffrey Dummer.

8th | 5th British Film and Television Awards (BAFTAS): "La Ronde" Best Film.

May

10th 5th Cannes Film Festival: "The Tragedy of Othello: The Moor of Venice" directed by Orson Welles and "Two Cents Worth of Hope" directed by Renato Castellani jointly awarded the Grand Prix du Festival International du Film.

13th Minor-league Bristol pitcher Ron Necciai strikes out 27 in 9-innings.

15th On the 15th May 1952, Johnny Longden became the first jockey in the United States to ride 4,000 winners and the second in the world to do so. (Two years earlier, Gordon Richards of England had achieved that feat.)

16th New Faces of 1952 is a musical revue with songs and comedy skits. The revue opened on Broadway at the Royale Theatre on the 16th May 1952 and ran for 365 performances. It was produced by Leonard Sillman, directed by John Murray Anderson and John Beal with choreography by Richard Barstow. The sketches were written by Graham and Brooks. The songs were composed by, among others, Harnick, Graham, Murray Grand and Arthur Siegel. The cast featured Graham, Kitt, Clary, Virginia Bosler, June Carroll, Virginia De Luce, Ghostley, Patricia Hammerlee, Lawrence, Lynde and Bill Milliken. De Luce and Graham won the 1952 Theatre World Award.

18th May 18th 1952: An analysis of the carbon-14 radioisotope in a piece of charred oak from an excavated pit at Stonehenge estimates that the mysterious structure on England's Salisbury Plain is 3,800 years old, plus or minus 275 years. The carbon-dating process that dated Stonehenge to about 1848 B.C. was conducted by the technique's godfather, Willard Libby.

Ann Davison was, at the age of 39, the first woman to single-handedly sail the Atlantic Ocean. She departed Plymouth, England in her 23-foot boat Felicity Ann on the 18th May 1952. She landed in Brittany, Portugal, Morocco and the Canary Islands, before setting sail across the Atlantic on the 20th November 1952, aiming to make land-fall in Antigua. In the event storms pushed her south and having been driven past Barbados she eventually touched land in Dominica on the 23rd January 1953. After an extended stopover in the Caribbean she sailed north to Florida and finally to New York.

May

21st | Dutch Queen Juliana opens Amsterdam-Rhine Canal.

27th | The Treaty establishing the European Defence Community, also known as the Treaty of Paris is an unratified treaty signed on the 27th May 1952 by the six 'inner' countries of European integration: the Benelux countries, France, Italy, and West Germany. The treaty would have created a European Defence Community (EDC) with a pan-European defence force. The treaty failed to obtain ratification in the French parliament and it was never ratified by Italy, so it consequently never entered into force. Instead, the London and Paris Conferences provided for West Germany's accession to NATO and the Western European Union (WEU, a largely dormant successor of the 1948 Western Union, WU, which had already been cannibalised by NATO).

28th | The Memphis Kiddie Park opened on the 28th May 1952. The park was one of several designed and opened by Stuart Wintner, who eventually closed all but the Memphis Kiddie Park to focus on his chain of indoor movie theatres. Though Mr. Wintner has since died, the park remains in operation and is owned by his son.

30th | Indianapolis 500: Troy Ruttman wins in 3:52:41.930 (207.480 km/h).

June

2nd | The 1952 steel strike was a strike by the United Steelworkers of America (USWA) against U.S. Steel (USS) and nine other steelmakers. The strike was scheduled to begin on the 9th April 1952, but US President Harry Truman nationalized the American steel industry hours before the workers walked out. The steel companies sued to regain control of their facilities. On the 2nd June 1952, in a landmark decision, the US Supreme Court ruled in Youngstown Sheet & Tube Co. v. Sawyer, 343 U.S. 579 (1952), that the President lacked the authority to seize the steel mills. The Steelworkers struck to win a wage increase. The strike lasted 53 days and ended on the 24th July 1952 on essentially the same terms that the union had proposed four months earlier.

June

5th	On the 7th June 1952 at Headingley, debutant Fred Trueman unleashed a spell from hell, and the Indian scoreboard at one stage read 0 for 4. ... When Fred Trueman had been called to the telephone at the RAF base and informed of his selection in the Test team, he was certain that it was a prank.
	Jersey Joe Walcott beats Ezzard Charles in 15 rounds for heavyweight boxing title.
7th	Curtis Cup Women's Golf, Muirfield, Scotland: Great Britain & Ireland score first ever win in the contest; beat US, 5-4.
11th	On the 11th June 1952 Len Hutton became the first professional cricketer of the 20th Century to captain England in Tests; under his captaincy England won the Ashes the following year for the first time in 19 years.
12th	The 2nd Berlin International Film Festival: "One Summer of Happiness" wins Golden Bear (audience vote).
13th	Soviet fighters shoot Swedish Dakota down over East Sea, kills 8.
14th	Nautilus's keel was laid at General Dynamics' Electric Boat Division in Groton, Connecticut by Harry S. Truman on the 14th June 1952. She was christened on the 21st January 1954 and launched into the Thames River.

16th	Soviet Fighters shoot Swedish Catalina reconnaissance flight down.
19th	The Special Forces (United States Army) are created.

June

21st | The Philippine School of Commerce, through a government act, is converted to the Philippine College of Commerce (later the Polytechnic University of the Philippines).

23rd | US airplanes bomb energy centres at Yalu Korea.

25th | PGA Championship Men's Golf, Big Spring CC: Jim Turnesa wins 1-up over Chick Harbert in the Wednesday final.

26th | The Pan-Malayan Labour Party is founded in Malaya, as a union of state wide labour parties.

27th | Decree 900 in Guatemala orders the redistribution of uncultivated land.

28th | The First Miss Universe was held. Armi Kuusela from Finland wins the title of Miss Universe 1952.

29th | US Open Women's Golf, Bala GC: 1949 champion Louise Suggs wins, 7 strokes ahead of runners-up Marlene Bauer and Betty Jameson.

30th | CBS announced Wednesday the cancellation of the longest-running scripted program in broadcasting history, the soap opera "Guiding Light." The show has been on radio and television for 72 years, beginning on NBC radio in 1937 and moving to CBS television on the 30th June 1952.

July

1st | The first NASCAR Grand National event is run outside of the US with Buddy Shuman winning the 200-lap race at Stamford Park, Ontario, Canada.

3rd | The ocean liner SS United States makes her maiden crossing of the Atlantic. The ship was the largest ocean liner constructed entirely in the United States and the fastest ocean liner to cross the Atlantic in either direction, retaining the Blue Riband for the highest average speed since her maiden voyage in 1952.

4th | Wimbledon Men's Tennis: Australian Frank Sedgman wins his only Wimbledon singles title beating Czech Jaroslav Drobný 4-6, 6-2, 6-3, 6-2.

Canadian Currency, Mint and Exchange Fund Act allow gold coins of $5, $10, and $20 to be minted.

July

5th   Wimbledon Women's Tennis: Maureen Connolly beats Louise Brough 7-5, 6-3 for the first of 3 straight Wimbledon crowns.

6th   The last tram journey in London for three decades took place between Woolwich and New Cross on the 6th July 1952.

7th   SS United States crosses Atlantic in record 82 hours and 40 mins.

11th   British Golf Men's Open, Royal Lytham & St Anne's GC: 3 titles in 4 years for Bobby Locke of South Africa beating Australian Peter Thomson by a stroke.

15th   1st transatlantic helicopter flight begins.

19th   The 1952 Summer Olympics opening ceremony, officially known as the Games of the XV Olympiad, were held at Helsinki in Finland. Helsinki was chosen as the host city over Amsterdam, Athens, Lausanne, and Stockholm and five American cities: Chicago, Detroit, Los Angeles, Minneapolis and Philadelphia. Helsinki had been given the 1940 Summer Olympics, but they were cancelled because of World War II.

20th   Emil Zatopek's won the 10,000m on the 20th July in an Olympic record of 29:17.0 and timed 14:06.6, another Olympic record in winning the 5000 four days later.

21st   The 1952 Kern County earthquake occurred on the 21st July in the southern San Joaquin Valley and measured 7.3 on the moment magnitude scale. The main shock occurred at 4:52 am Pacific Daylight Time (11:52 UTC), killed 12 people and injured hundreds, and caused an estimated $60 million in property damage.

24th   US President Harry Truman settles 53-day steel strike.

     "High Noon", American Western film directed by Fred Zinnemann, starring Gary Cooper and Thomas Mitchell, is released.

July

26th | Argentine First Lady Eva Peron dies of cancer at age 33 and goes on to achieve saintly status in Argentina.

27th | Swedish race walker John Mikaelsson makes it back-to-back gold medals in the 10k event at the Helsinki Olympics, having won the corresponding race in London in 1948.

30th | Ford Frick sets waiver rule to bar inter-league deals until all clubs in same league get right to bid.

August

2nd | 17 year-old future world champion Floyd Patterson wins the gold medal in the middleweight division at the Helsinki Olympic Games with a 1st round KO of Romanian Vasile Tita.

3rd | Italian Ferrari driver Alberto Ascari clinches Formula 1 World Drivers Championship by winning German Grand Prix at the Nürburgring.

XV Summer Olympic Games close in Helsinki, Finland.

4th | Gambling boss Theodore Roe is murdered by the crew of Sam Giancana.

6th | The Treaty of Taipei between Japan and the Republic of China goes into effect, to officially end the Second Sino-Japanese War.

9th | General strike against overtime conscription in Belgium.

11th | The Jordanian Parliament forces King Talal of Jordan to abdicate due to mental illness; he is succeeded by his son King Hussein.

12th | The Night of the Murdered Poets was the execution of thirteen Soviet Jews in the Lubyanka Prison in Moscow, Russian SFSR, Soviet Union on 12 August 1952. The arrests were first made in September 1948 and June 1949. All defendants were falsely accused of espionage and treason as well as many other crimes. After their arrests, they were tortured, beaten, and isolated for three years before being formally charged. There were five Yiddish writers among these defendants, all of whom were part of the Jewish Anti-Fascist Committee.

15th | On the 15th and 16th August 1952, a storm of tropical intensity broke over South West England, depositing 229 millimetres (9.0 in) of rain within 24 hours on an already waterlogged Exmoor. It is thought that a cold front scooped up a thunderstorm, and the orographic effect worsened the storm. Debris-laden floodwaters cascaded down the northern escarpment of the moor, converging upon the village of Lynmouth. In particular, in the upper West Lyn valley, a dam was formed by fallen trees and other debris; this in due course gave way, sending a huge wave of water and debris down that river. The River Lyn through the town had been culverted in order to gain land for business premises; this culvert soon choked with flood debris, and the river flowed through the town. Much of the debris was boulders and trees.

20th | 13th Venice Film Festival: "Genghis Khan" directed by Manuel Conde wins the Golden Lion.

22nd | The penal colony on Devil's Island is permanently closed.

August

22nd The most damaging shock of the 1952 Kern County earthquake sequence strikes with a moment magnitude of 5.8, and a maximum Mercalli intensity of VIII (Severe). This event damages several hundred buildings in Bakersfield, California, with total additional losses of $10 million, with two associated deaths and some injuries.

23rd Kitty Wells becomes the first woman to score a number 1 hit on the American country charts, with the song "It Wasn't God Who Made Honky Tonk Angels".

26th A British passenger jet makes a return crossing of the Atlantic Ocean in the same day.

27th Having already won 5,000m and 10,000m gold medals, Czech star Emil Zátopek claims rare Olympic treble taking out Helsinki Games marathon in OR 2:23:03.2.

Reparation negotiations between West Germany and Israel end in Luxembourg: Germany will pay 3 billion Deutsche Marks.

29th Composer John Cage's 4'33", during which the performer does not play, premieres in Woodstock, New York.

30th The last Finnish war reparations are sent to the Soviet Union.

31st The Grenzlandring racetrack closes in Wegberg, Germany. The Grenzlandring, too many foreigners also known as Wegbergring or Wegberg-Ring, is told to be "discovered" nearly undamaged after World War II when during one dark night in 1947, Dr. Carl Marcus, town mayor of nearby Rheydt, drove along a more or less straight looking country road. When he passed a bicycle rider more than once, he suddenly realized that this road must be a full circle. In fact, a 9 km (5.6 mi) long and 6.8 m (22 ft) wide egg-shaped concrete ring road had been built before World War II around Wegberg and the neighbouring village of Beeck and completed in 1938 or 1939, at total cost of about 3.3 million Reichsmark. As it was intended for military purposes, the construction had not made been public nor was the road shown on maps. This story today is considered part of a marketing strategy since parts of the ring had been used by US and British military immediately after the war and had in no way been unknown.

September

2nd Dr. C. Walton Lillehei and Dr. F. John Lewis perform the first open-heart surgery, at the University of Minnesota.

6th Television debuts in Canada, as the CBC in Montreal, Quebec airs.

7th NY Yankees Johnny Mize's pinch-hit grand slam gives Yanks a 5-1 win at Washington, giving him a HR in all 15 major league parks.

Alberto Ascari of Italy in a Ferrari wins Formula 1 World Drivers Championship with victory in season ending Italian Grand Prix at Monza; wins title by 12 points from countryman Giuseppe Farina.

8th Ernest Hemingway's novel "The Old Man & the Sea" published.

September

8th US National Championship Men's Tennis, Forest Hills, NY: Australian Frank Sedgman wins his second straight US title; beats American Gardnar Mulloy 6-1, 6-2, 6-3; last amateur major before turning pro in 1953.

US National Championship Women's Tennis, Forest Hills, NY: Defending champion Maureen Connolly beats fellow American Doris Hart 6-3, 7-5.

11th West German Chancellor Konrad Adenauer signs a reparation pact for the Jewish people.

12th Noël Coward's "Quadrille," premieres in London.

17th "I am an American Day" & "Constitution Day" renamed "Citizenship Day".

19th "Adventures of Superman" TV series starring George Reeves premieres in syndication in the US.

19th The United States bars Charlie Chaplin from re-entering the country after a trip to England.

23rd 1st closed circuit pay-tv telecast of a sports event.

Undefeated Rocky Marciano KOs defending champion Jersey Joe Walcott in the 13th round at Municipal Stadium, Philadelphia for the world heavyweight boxing title.

24th American fast food restaurant chain "KFC" [Kentucky Fried Chicken] opens its first franchise in Salt Lake City, Utah.

28th St. Louis Cardinals outfielder Stan Musial makes his only major league pitching appearance, throwing one pitch to Chicago Cubs Frank Baumholtz.

30th The Revised Standard Version of the Bible is published.

October

2nd | Don Liddle beats Bob Lemon 7-4 as the New York Giants complete an unlikely Baseball World Series sweep of the powerful Cleveland Indians; Cleveland season record of 111-43 sets American League mark for regular season wins.

3rd | 1st British nuclear test during Operation Hurricane at Monte Bello Island, Australia, UK becomes the world's third nuclear nation.

4th | "Top Banana" closes at Winter Garden Theatre NYC after 356 performances.

5th | 6th NHL All-Star Game, Detroit Olympia, Detroit, MI: 1st Team ties 2nd Team, 1-1; second year format - 1st v 2nd All-Star Teams, with additional players.

6th | Agatha Christie's play "The Mousetrap" opens in London (still running).
The Mousetrap is a murder mystery play by Agatha Christie. The Mousetrap opened in London's West End in October 6th 1952 and ran continuously until 16th March 2020, when the stage performances had to be discontinued due to the COVID-19 pandemic.

A poster of Ambassador Theatre
in London playing
and playing
and playing ...the Mousetrap

2 Agatha's photographs
in different time periods.

Rare Coward's telegram
to Agatha Christie
located at Ambassador Theatre
in London!

The first DELL
publication
of Mousetrap

7th | First "Bandstand" broadcast in Philadelphia on WFIL-TV (Dick Clark joins in 1955 as a substitute-host).

8th | It was a foggy morning on the 8th October 1952, when a train speeding from Perth to Euston smashed into the back of a parked train at platform six of Harrow and Wealdstone station. ... The tragedy killed 112 people and injured 300 more and to date is the most catastrophic train crash to happen during peace time in England.

14th | The United Nations begins work in the new United Nations building in New York City, designed by Le Corbusier and Oscar Niemeyer.

15th | "Charlotte's Web" by E. B. White and illustrated by Garth Williams is published by Harper & Brothers.

Henri Cartier-Bresson's influential photography book "The Decisive Moment" is first published in the US and France.

16th | Woolworth's at Powell & Market (San Francisco) opens.

18th | Mad magazine was founded on the 18th October 1952 as a comic book, the first issue written almost entirely by its editor Harvey Kurtzman. It became a magazine in 1955 and soon began building up influence and readership with its sharp satire and cheerful daftness.

19th | Alain Bombard departs from the Canary Islands on his solitary journey across the Atlantic ocean with almost no provisions and only a sextant for navigation to test his theory that a shipwrecked person could survive.

23rd | "Limelight" premieres directed, written, produced and starring Charlie Chaplin and Claire Bloom with appearance by Buster Keaton.

October

25th In 1952, Walt Disney's Donald Duck, already known through animations, introduced the first Dutch Donald Duck weekly magazine. The first issue was distributed for free on the 25th October 1952, and immediately became a great success. Donald Duck Weekly is still going strong and has celebrated its 60th birthday in 2012.

27th "My Darlin' Aida" opens at Winter Garden Theatre NYC for 89 performances.

30th Clarence Birdseye sells first frozen peas.

November

1st Nuclear testing and Operation Ivy: The United States successfully detonates the first hydrogen bomb, codenamed "Mike", at Eniwetok Atoll in the Marshall Islands in the central Pacific Ocean, with a yield of 10.4 megatons.

4th Pace-Finletter MOU 1952: A Memorandum of understanding is signed between "...Air Force Secretary Finletter and Army Secretary Pace that established a fixed wing weight limit [for the Army] of five thousand pounds empty, but weight restrictions on helicopters were eliminated..."

10th Trygve Lie resigns as 1st Secretary General of the United Nations.

12th White Sox place Jim Rivera on 1 year probation after cleared of rape.

14th The first Singles Chart is published in the New Music Express, dated Friday 14th November. It is published as a Top 12, although it comprises 15 singles - because of ties at Number 7, Number 8 and Number 11. The Number 1 is Al Martino's Here In My Heart and the first Number 2 is Jo Stafford's You Belong To Me.

19th The F-86A set its first official world speed record of 671 miles per hour (1,080 km/h) on September 15th 1948 at Muroc Dry Lake, flown by Major Richard L. Johnson, USAF. Five years later, on the 18th May 1953, Jacqueline Cochran became the first woman to break the sound barrier, flying a "one-off" Canadian-built F-86 Sabre Mk 3, alongside Chuck Yeager.

November

20th | The first official passenger flight over the North Pole is made, from Los Angeles to Copenhagen.

21st | 1st US postage stamp in 2 colours (rotary process) introduced.

26th | 1st 3D feature film "Bwana Devil" directed by Arch Oboler premieres in Los Angeles, advertised as "The Miracle of the Age!!! A LION in your lap! A LOVER in your arms!"

29th | CFL Grey Cup, Varsity Stadium, Toronto: Toronto Argonauts prove to be the dominant club in Canada with their record 10th Championship; beat Edmonton Eskimos, 21-11.

Korean War: U.S. President-elect Dwight D. Eisenhower fulfils a political campaign promise, by traveling to Korea to find out what can be done to end the conflict.

December

1st | The New York Daily News carries a front-page story announcing that Christine Jorgensen, a transsexual woman in Denmark, has become the recipient of the first successful sexual reassignment operation.

2nd | Today in Heritage History, 1952, for the very first time ever, a human birth is televised by educational channel KOA-TV in Denver, Colorado. KOA assured the birth mother that her face would at no time be shown during the broadcast. They did however, run a "Guess Who's the Mystery Vagina" promotion and phone-in contest asking for station subscriber donations, during the shows airing. The Grand Prize winner received an all-expense paid historical trip for two to Virgin City, Wyoming. Oddly and of special note, the Grand Prize winner turned-out to be someone other than the "mystery" vagina's husband, and coincidentally (also) the main Cameraman.

4th | Walter P. Reuther chosen chairman of the Congress of Industrial Organizations (CIO) in the US.

5th | The worst smog in London ever, 4-8,000 die.

14th | The first successful surgical separation of Siamese twins is conducted in Mount Sinai Hospital, Cleveland, Ohio.

UN Troops kill 82 North Korean POWs during a prison camp riot in Pongam-do, South Korea.

15th | KHON TV channel 2 in Honolulu, HI (NBC) begins broadcasting.

18th | Ellis W Ryan resigns as Cleveland Indians president.

20th | The 1952 Moses Lake C-124 crash was an accident in which a United States Air Force Douglas C-124 Globemaster II military transport aircraft crashed near Moses Lake, Washington on December 20th 1952. Of the 115 people on board, 87 died and 28 survived. The crash was the world's deadliest aviation disaster involving a single aircraft at the time, surpassing the Llandow air disaster, which killed 80 people. The death toll would not be surpassed until the Tachikawa air disaster, which also involved a Douglas C-124A-DL Globemaster II, killed 129 people.

December

21st Broadway Tunnel opens in San Francisco. The final cost was some $7.3 million (equivalent to $57.5 million in 2019). Completion was originally projected for May 1952, but unanticipated loose rock meant that shoring was required. The tunnel opened to traffic on December 21st 1952.

23rd Alain Bombard arrives in Barbados after 65 days at sea proving his theory that a shipwrecked person could survive with almost no provisions, despite having lost 25 kg (65 lbs) in weight.

25th One West German soldier is killed, in a shooting incident in West Berlin.

26th Joseph Ivor Linton, the first Israeli Minister Plenipotentiary in Japan, presents his credentials to the Emperor of Japan.

28th National Football League Championship, Cleveland Municipal Stadium: Detroit Lions beat Cleveland Browns, 17-7.

31st Danny Nardico stops former world middleweight champion Jake LaMotta in 7 rounds in a light heavyweight non-title bout in Coral Gables, Florida; LaMotta is knocked down for the only time in his career, his corner stopping fight after the round.

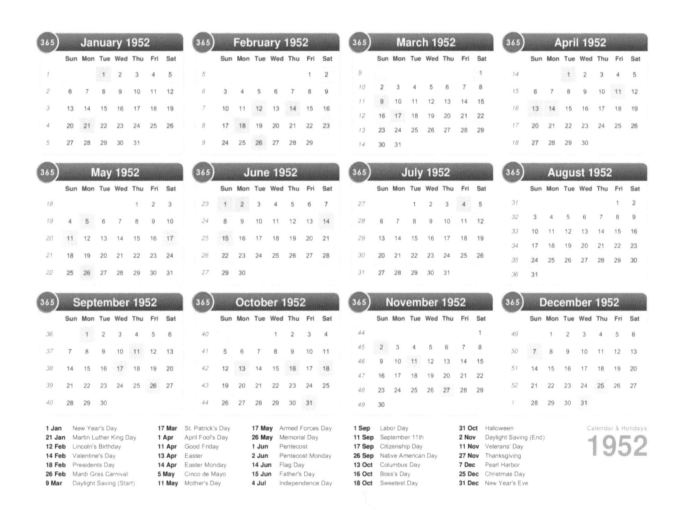

PEOPLE IN POWER

Robert Menzies
1949-1966
Australia
Prime Minister

Vincent Auriol
1947-1954
France
Président

Getúlio Vargas
1951-1954
Brazil
President

Louis St. Laurent
1948-1957
Canada
Prime Minister

Mao Zedong
1943-1976
China
Government of China

Theodor Heuss
1949-1959
Germany
President of Germany

Rajendra Prasad
1950-1962
India
1st President of India

Luigi Einaudi
1948-1955
Italy
President

Hiroito
1926-1989
Japan
Emperor

Miguel Alemán Valdés
1946-1952
Mexico
46th President of Mexico

Joseph Stalin
1922-1952
Russia
Premier

D. F. Malan
1948-1954
South Africa
Prime Minister

Harry S. Truman
1945-1953
United States
President

Joseph Pholien
1950-1952
Belgium
Prime Minister

Sidney Holland
1949-1957
New Zealand
Prime Minister

Sir Winston Churchill
1951-1955
United Kingdom
Prime Minister

Tage Erlander
1946-1969
Sweden
Prime Minister

Erik Eriksen
1950-1953
Denmark
Prime Minister

Francisco Franco
1936-1975
Spain
President

Mátyás Rákosi
1948-1956
Hungary
Hungarian Working
People's Party

The Year You Were Born 1952
Book by Sapphire Publishing

Printed in Great Britain
by Amazon

12034567R00045